DARFUR TO
TAIPEI

CASES IN FOREIGN POLICY ANALYSIS

Edited by:

Edelgard Mahant

Daniel Bodistean

Toronto, Glendon College, January 2015

INTRODUCTION

The papers in this book span the entire gamut of the foreign policy process, from the inputs of the interest groups and social movements that attempt to influence a state's foreign policy to the negotiations that try to bring about international agreements to the actions governments take as they attempt to achieve their foreign policy objectives.

The first three papers focus on inputs. Neena Sethi's paper on environmental groups and American foreign policy consists of original research that tries to show to what extent these groups can sometimes succeed in influencing U.S. foreign policy. Daniel Bodistean's paper on the Canadian-American negotiations on the Keystone pipeline uses game theory to analyze these negotiations. It is of continuing relevance because, as of this writing, we still do not know whether the cross border segment of the pipeline will ever be built. Alexandra Pullano's paper on the EEC/EU's policy toward the negotiations with Turkey introduces a fascinating mixture of economic self-interest and identity politics on the part of the EU.

The next section of the book deals with foreign policy objectives. Sarah Frion uses discourse analysis to determine the extent to which the U.S. and France drew on their foreign policy to try and enhance their domestic security in the post-9/11 climate. Easha Acharya deals with the newest aspect of national security, cyber-security. She explores the problems some countries have faced when they were the target of cyber-attacks, then explores possible measures governments could take to protect their cyber installations, using the U.S. as a model. So this paper is prescriptive as well as analytical.

A third section deals with the challenges faced by the foreign policy makers of middle powers, a problem already mentioned by Acharya. Emily Preston demonstrates how, in the case of Darfur, the Canadian government did not live up to the policy of the "responsibility to protect" that it proclaimed less than a decade earlier. The other paper in this section also deals with human security; Marie-Pascale Poku finds that the African middle powers have been no more successful than has Canada in contributing to human security on the continent.

The last section consists of four papers on various aspects of American foreign policy. Ashley Walcott writes about the process of decision-making in the early days of the Clinton administration and traces the effect that the inexperience of that administration had on the decision to send American aid and soldiers to Somalia. Saquib Ahsan uses a neo-Gramscian framework to analyse the Taiwan Relations Act as a component of U.S. policy toward the two Chinas. He identifies a policy he labels as cultural hegemony. He uses a similar approach as he analyses U.S. policy in Latin America. He finds that while George W. Bush's policy had a harsher tone than that of Barrack Obama, the ultimate objective, that of reducing the influence of the Latin American Left, has remained the same. Daniel Bodistean's final paper uses a methodology similar to that used by Ahsan. He traces the effectiveness of the various means of foreign policy implementation that American administrations used as they sought to influence the government of Libya's policies on issues such as terrorism and nuclear weapons and finds that, in the end, these policies have been quite successful.

The papers in this volume use a number of theoretical approaches from liberalism in the Morvacsik sense of the word

(Sethi) to rational choice (Bodistean) to discourse analysis (Frion) and neo-Gramscianism (Ahsan) to decision-making (Frion). Interestingly, two of the contributors (Preston and Poku) use the human security framework, which the Canadian government helped to introduce on the international scene. Although Acharya's paper is about the protection of national security and Frion's about the effect of international events on domestic security, none of the young writers have chosen the traditional realist framework, which was not so long ago the hallmark of international relations. Perhaps this small sample gives a glimpse of the future of theories of foreign policy.

Altogether, these eleven papers consist of much original research and new points of view on the making and implementation of foreign policy. We hope that they will inspire other undergraduates to do likewise!

Daniel Bodistean

Edelgard Mahant

Acknowledgements

This book would not be possible without the technical knowhow and guidance of Professor Xavier de Vanssay. His help with the technical side of things has truly made the book come to reality. Further acknowledgement is owed to Karin Jurgens for her help with the graphic design of the book. Finally, each individual author within this book is owed acknowledgement for their diligence in preparing their papers for this project.

CONTENTS

FOREIGN POLICY MAKING

1. ENVIRONMENTAL INTEREST GROUPS & U.S. FOREIGN POLICY

A CASE STUDY OF THE NATIONAL RESOURCES DEFENSE COUNCIL (NRDC)
By: Neena Sethi

Introduction

Global environmental problems are truly transnational and require transnational solutions. States, large and small, are not beyond the impacts of contemporary environmental problems such as climate change or changes to the marine environment. All states contribute to the problem to some degree. The existence of international conventions and regimes on the environment suggests that states are aware that changes to the environment due to human activity must be addressed by states. As with many domains that fall under state jurisdiction, how and why a state decides to address the environment in international society are questions with complex answers.

One aspect of state behaviour in international society examines the role environmental interest groups play in influencing foreign policy on the environment. This paper intends to examine the influence of environmental interest groups on U.S. foreign policy behaviour; specifically, the activities of one particular environmental interest group, the National Resources Defense Council (NRDC). Do the activities of the NRDC push the U.S. government to act as a lead state in the foreign policy environment? I hypothesize that the activities of the NRDC do not consistently push the U.S. government to act as a lead state in the foreign policy environment.

NRDC Profile:

The National Resources Defense Council (NRDC) considers itself to be the most effective environmental action organization in the United States (NRDC, 2012a, About). Founded by a group of law students and attorneys in 1970, they have 1.4 million members and online activists (NRDC, 2012b, About NRDC/Who we are). Although the membership does not represent a significant or remarkable percentage of the American population, the NRDC has managed to become a strong voice for environmental issues. Perhaps one of its most significant victories came in 1986 when they won "passage of legislation requiring the U.S. government to set up 'early warning system' to track environmentally harmful multilateral bank projects" (NRDC, 2012d, About/Victories Archive). This legislation requires environmental NGOs and representatives from the Treasury, State Department, USAID, and the Environmental Protection Agency to review upcoming environmentally controversial loans to Multilateral Development Banks (MDBs) on a monthly basis (Bøås, 2001, 184). The NRDC takes credit for this legislation; their members drafted the legislation that was passed in cooperation with the Sierra Club (Bøås, 2001, 184).

The NRDC focuses on creating legislative changes, both federally and at the state level so that state agencies and departments require private industries to take the long-term health and welfare of present and future generations into consideration (NRDC, 2012c, About/Mission Statement). In this way, the NRDC works to increase the transparency of practices of private industry as it is the right of all people to have a voice in decisions that affect their environment" (NRDC, 2013c, About/Mission Statement).

The NRDC focuses on six priorities:

1. Curbing Global Warming and Creating the Clean Energy Future
2. Reviving the World's Oceans
3. Defending Endangered Wildlife and Wild Places
4. Protecting Our Health by Preventing Pollution
5. Ensuring Safe and Sufficient Water
6. Fostering Sustainable Communities

(NRDC, 2013, About)

Each priority has several different projects. Not all projects have an international focus or attempt to influence U.S. foreign policy. In fact, the majority of NRDC projects appear to be focused on domestic issues. The commonality in all of the NRDC's projects is that they seek to collaborate with government and help create sound environmental policy.

Methodology

While it may be impossible to definitively say that an interest group influences the foreign policy decisions of a government, when undertaking a study of a particular interest group, the evidence can strongly suggest whether this influence exists or not. In developing a methodology for this research, I looked to connect NRDC activities with U.S. foreign policy behaviour by constructing a timeline (from inception to result) for different case studies. These case studies were identified by applying a set of criteria to isolate activities of the NRDC intention to influence U.S. foreign policy behavior. For each case study, I linked official U.S. communications and NRDC communications and created a timeline. Analyses of the communications within the timeline suggest if U.S foreign policy responded to activities of the NRDC.

Independent Variable

To begin my analysis, I first identified appropriate case studies. I identified two different sources from the NRDC: 1) the 2011 NRDC Annual Report and 2) NRDC "victories" as identified on their website. Annual Reports are an official way in which a private entity communicates its accomplishments to its membership and to the general public; the 2011 Annual Report was the only such report available to the public on the NRDC website. I used the NRDC "victories" page on the NRDC website as well, as this is also a way in which the organization communicates its accomplishments. Using these two sources, I applied several filters to capture a set of case studies, that were international in nature:

1. Time – I opted to review a three year period so that I could capture a sufficient number of case studies. I used the 2011 Annual Report as my starting point and then included "victories" from 2012 and 2013 as identified on the NRDC website

2. International Organizations – a case study was considered to be international if the NRDC identified that they were working with an international organization or seeking to influence the decision making or policy of an international organization

3. Member of a U.S. Delegation – a case study was considered to be international if the NRDC identified themselves as a member of the U.S. delegation to an international organization

After applying these filters, I identified five (5) NRDC case studies that I could use to conduct my analysis. I relied on NRDC press releases and blog posts from their staff blog, *Switchboard*, to capture additional evidence of their activities to influence U.S.

foreign policy behavior for each case study.

Dependent Variable

My dependent variable focused on resulting U.S. foreign policy behaviour on the five NRDC case studies. There are several ways a state's foreign policy behaviour can be observed: press releases, as they are addressed to the international and domestic community (Mahant 2012); and other official communications like presidential memorandums and directives; congressional hearings, legislation, and participation in conventions and treaties – these can define the scope of interaction between domestic and foreign entities.

Categorization Of Results

Evidence of state behaviour can be indicative of the role that a state plays in international society. Porter and Brown (1996, 32-33) describe the roles and interests of state actors relating to the process of environmental regime formation:

> In negotiations, a state actor may play one of four possible roles: lead state, supporting state, swing state, veto or blocking state.

> When a big power like the United States takes a lead role, it helps to sway states that do not otherwise have clearly defined interests on an issue.

Bøås (2001, 182) attempted to understand the influence of the NGO community on United States environmental foreign policy. Using the roles, as described by Porter and Brown (1996), Bøås sought to determine if the NGO community could push the United States to act as a lead state instead of as a swing state or veto/blocking state in its foreign environmental policy.

ROLE	DEFINITION
Lead State	Strong commitment to effective international action on an issue, moves the process of negotiation forward, attempts to get the support of other states
Supporting State	Speaks in favour of the proposal of a lead state in negotiations
Swing State	Demands significant concessions to its interests as a price for going along with an agreement
Blocking State	Opposes a proposed regime outright or tries to weaken it to the point that it cannot be effective

Specifically, Bøås traced the NGOs' path to influence through various branches of government and directly through multilateral development banks (MDBs) (2001, 182).

Building on what is presented by Porter and Brown (1996) and Bøås (2001), I decided to categorize my results based on whether the U.S. acted as a Lead State, Supporting State, Swing State or Blocking State for each of the five NRDC case studies.

Summary Of Results

A summary of my results precedes a detailed description of each case study which led to the conclusion of the U.S. role in foreign environment policy as described below. Each case study is involved with an international organization and a policy outcome.

CASE STUDY	INTERNATIONAL ORGANIZATION	POLICY OUTCOME	U.S. ROLE
1	International Whaling Commission (IWC)	Strengthen transparency and overall effectiveness of IWC	Supporting State
2	United Nations (UN)	Convention on the Conservation and Management of High Seas Fisheries Resources in the North Pacific Ocean	Lead State
3	United Nations Environment Program (UNEP)	Elimination of lead gasoline globally	Supporting State
4	International Maritime Organization (IMO)	Global GHG reduction regime for the shipping industry	Blocking State
5	World Bank	No funding for coal power projects	Lead State

Case One: International Whaling Commission (IWC) And Commercial Whaling

In 1986, the IWC imposed a moratorium on commercial whaling, a moratorium which is binding on member states (IWC, 2013, Commercial Whaling). Although Iceland and Norway are member states of the IWC, they both engage in commercial whaling, either under objection to the moratorium decision or under reservation to it (IWC, 2013, Commercial Whaling). Iceland specifically resumed its commercial whaling in 2006 (Kiekow, 2013); at that time the NRDC began a campaign to pressure the U.S. government to pressure Iceland into abandoning its commercial whaling industry.

The first evidence of U.S. foreign policy behaviour in regards to Iceland's commercial whaling appeared in 2009, when the U.S. Department of State issued a press release in opposition to Iceland's decision to establish a large commercial whaling quota. The release announced that the United States was deeply concerned that whale stocks were not adequate to support the harvest proposed by Iceland (U.S. Department of State, 2009). The press release further called on the Government of Iceland to rescind its decision and focus on long-term conservation of whale stocks so as not to undermine the ongoing efforts of the IWC (U.S. Department of State, 2009). By 2010, the U.S. Government changed its position by voicing support for a proposal to overturn the international moratorium in favour of regulations such as setting catch limits (NRDC, 2010). The NRDC quickly mobilized and filed a petition with the U.S. Departments of Commerce and of the Interior to impose trade sanctions against Iceland and to invoke the Pelly Amendment of the Fisherman's Protective Act (Kiekow, 2010). The Pelly Amendment "authorizes the President to impose trade sanctions against another country for 'diminishing the effectiveness' of conservation agreements: in

Iceland's case, the International Convention for the Regulation of Whaling" (Kiekow, 2010) that bans commercial whaling. Once the amendment is invoked by the Department of Commerce or Department of Interior, the President has sixty days to decide whether or not to impose sanctions (Maroney, 2013). The U.S. government didn't invoke the Pelly Amendment and it did not impose sanctions; the proposal to overturn the moratorium was also not passed.

In their 2011 Annual Report, the NRDC reported that they were invited to be a member of the U.S. delegation at the 2011 annual meeting of the International Whaling Commission and represented the interests of NGOs at that meeting(NRDC, 2011, 11). According to the report, prior to that IWC meeting, the NRDC mobilized its members to escalate pressure on the Obama Administration who in turn imposed diplomatic sanctions on Iceland (NRDC, 2011, 11). The NRDC's objective was to influence the U.S. to impose tough economic sanctions on Icelandic seafood companies with direct ties to the whaling industry (NRDC, 2011, 11), thereby forcing Iceland to abandon commercial whaling. This objective was not reached as the U.S. did not recommend sanctions at that meeting, but rather, took on the role of a supporting state to pass a U.K. sponsored resolution "aimed at strengthening transparency and the overall effectiveness of the IWC" (NRDC, 2011, 11). Immediately following the IWC annual meeting, the Secretary of Commerce, Gary Locke did invoke the Pelly Amendment, recommending several possible actions that the President could take (Locke, 2011). The NRDC suggests that Locke's declaration was in direct response to the petition from 2010 (Kiekow, 2011). But Locke's recommendations did not suggest that the President pursue economic sanctions; instead Locke suggested that the President continue with diplomatic pressure and sanctions. The President received Locke's recommendations and in September issued a Memorandum to all Departments with Locke's recommendations and further directed the Departments to "keep the situation under review and to continue to urge Iceland to cease its commercial whaling activities" (Obama, 2011).

The result of this case study: the U.S. did not act as a lead state to stop commercial whaling by Iceland; instead, it acted as a supporting state of a U.K. resolution to increase the transparency and effectiveness of the IWC. But the actual situation of Icelandic commercial whaling did not change. The NRDC did not achieve their objective of ending commercial whaling via economic sanctions imposed on Iceland by the U.S.

Case Two: United Nations And Bottom Trawling

In April 2013, President Obama presented the Convention on the Conservation and Management of High Seas Fisheries Resources in the North Pacific Ocean to the United States Senate for ratification. The treaty creates a Commission with a mandate to implement, monitor and enforce restrictions on fisheries in the North Pacific Ocean. In their 2011 Annual Report, the NRDC credited itself as "laying the ground work for this historic victory back in 2006 when, armed with the best available scientific evidence, we helped convince the U.N. to pass a resolution calling on fishing nations to stop unregulated bottom trawling" (NRDC, 2011, 8). This was UN G.A Resolution A/RES/61/105 on sustainable fisheries. After the passing of the resolution, the NRDC suggest that with "steady pressure and rigorous oversight by NRDC and our partners, the world's leading fishing nations signed a landmark treaty to protect more than 16 million square miles of the Pacific Ocean from unregulated, destructive, bottom trawling" (NRDC, 2011, 8). The steady pressure occurred over the period of 2007-2011.

The NRDC first reported their involvement in the campaign to eliminate bottom trawling in 2007. The NRDC reported that it, along with other environmental groups, were "pressing the United Nations General Assembly and international fisheries management authorities to adopt an immediate moratorium on unregulated trawling in international waters" (NRDC, 2007). The NRDC were able to address the General Assembly due to their consultative status at the United Nations (granted in 1973); this status permits the NRDC and other NGOs to make occasional and useful contributions to the Economic and Social Council (ECOSOC) at the U.N. (United Nations Department of Economic and Social Affairs, 2013). It also provides NGO access to the General Assembly. Consultative Status establishes a working relationship between an NGO and the U.N. Secretariat who often work in tandem to persuade governments on policy formulation priorities (Willetts, 1996). Willetts (1996) suggests that:

> The best situation for an NGO can be to find a delegation [...] work together on drafting proposals which are tabled by the government. Intergovernmental negotiations will usually be dominated by official delegations, but that does not exclude the possibility of significant NGO influence behind the scenes.

In addition to their address to the General Assembly, in their 2011 Annual Report, the NRDC identified themselves as a member of the U.S. delegation involved in drafting the Convention on the Conservation and Management of High Seas Fisheries Resources in the North Pacific Ocean. "We worked closely with the State Department and other conservations groups [...] gradually, a strongly worded treat began to take shape"

(NRDC, 2011, 8). In 2012 the U.S. signed the Convention on the Conservation and Management of High Seas Fisheries Resources in the North Pacific Ocean.

The result of this case study: the U.S. did take the role of the Lead State. The NRDC's inclusion as a member to the U.S. delegation and the presentation of a signed treaty to the U.S. Senate for ratification in 2013 do suggest NRDC influence on U.S. foreign policy behavior.

Case Three: United Nations Environment Program (UNEP) And Leaded Gasoline

The campaign to phase out leaded gasoline was one of the first causes the NRDC undertook. This campaign started out as a domestic undertaking, challenging the inaction of the U.S. Environmental Protection Agency (EPA),

> When the EPA stalled on regulating lead emissions, a very young NRDC took up the cause. In 1973, an NRDC lawsuit resulted in the first EPA rules to regulate lead in gasoline. By 1978, after several years of battling in the courts and fighting pushback from industry, the phase out of lead from vehicle fuel in the United States had begun.
> (Lehner, 2011)

This case became international in 1992, when the NRDC began to push for a global phase out of leaded gasoline. After surveying nations around the world about leaded gas use, the NRDC presented its findings to the United Nations Commission on Sustainable Development which agreed to call for a global phase-out (Lehner, 2011).

U.S. Foreign Policy behavior on this issue was low-key;

their support of this initiative is evidenced in their membership in the 2002 Partnership for Clean Fuels and Vehicles under the UNEP. However, the lack of foreign policy evidence in the form of signed treaties or press releases suggests that the U.S. did not do much to move the process forward. The NRDC is one of the founding members of the Partnership for Clean Fuels and Vehicles and worked with several governments, industry leaders and environmental organizations from all over the world (Lehner, 2011). A 99% global phase out of leaded gasoline was announced by the NRDC in 2011 (Lehner, 2011). There were no press releases, declarations or announcements found from the State Department or the EPA to suggest that the U.S. government took a leadership role in the global phase out of leaded gasoline. The result of this case study: the lack of official state and state agency communications suggests that the U.S. played the role of a supporting state in this case , i.e. they did not oppose the global phase out of leaded gasoline; they simply supported the effort.

Case Four: International Maritime Organization (IMO), Emission Control Areas (ECA) And Greenhouse Gases (GHG)

In October of 2008, the member states of the IMO adopted new standards to control exhaust emissions from ocean vessel engines (United States Environmental Protection Agency, 2008). From the beginning, the U.S. took a leadership role to implement these standards. "The United States Environmental Protection Agency (EPA), in partnership with the Coast Guard, Navy, National Oceanic and Atmospheric Administration, Maritime Administration and State Department, played a significant role in the complex negotiations leading up to this agreement" (United States Environmental Protection Agency, 2008). The agreement focused on controlling emissions of ocean vessels within Emission Control Areas (ECA). An ECA is the area within 200 nautical miles of a coast (Kassel, 2010a). Upon entering an ECA, an ocean vessel would be required to use fuel that emitted 98% less sulfur than current ship fuel and 80% nitrogen oxide (Kassel, 2010a). The IMO defined the regulations for the emission controls by July 2010; the NRDC identified itself as a member of the 2010 U.S. delegation to the IMO that pushed for the adoption of this program in their 2011 Annual Report (NRDC, 2011, 5).

Initially, the EPA and the NRDC were on the same page with the outcome of this proposal. All ocean vessels were to reduce their engine emissions in a phase out approach. Some of the highest emissions of ocean vessels contain up to 45,000 parts-per-million (ppm) of sulfur (Kassel, 2010a). Within ECAs, ocean vessels were to emit no more than 10,000 ppm of sulfur as of July 2010; by January 2015, ocean vessels were to emit no more than 1,000 ppm of sulfur; by January 2016 an 80% reduction in nitrogen oxide emissions (United States Environmental Protection Agency, 2008). The EPA viewed this as a way to control the emissions of foreign-flagged vessels that outnumbered U.S. flagged vessels in U.S. ports (United States Environmental Protection Agency, 2008). Essentially, the EPA attributed U.S. air quality problems, especially in port cities, to the emissions from foreign-flagged vessels; the healthcare and welfare related costs amounted to billions of dollars (United States Environmental Protection Agency, 2008). The NRDC applauded U.S. leadership to implement ECAs and viewed this as a significant environmental victory (Kassel, 2010a).

By September 2010, the U.S. position had significantly changed. The NRDC reported that the U.S. put forth a proposal to exempt all steamships from emission controls within ECAs (Kassel, 2010b). In addition to compromising the vision of the original ECA proposal, the NRDC said that steamship exemption would provide a competitive advantage to the companies that use the oldest, dirtiest ships (Kassel, 2010b). The U.S. change of position was attributed to economics, retrofitting ships takes time, equipment, money and training of ship workers (Kassel, 2010c). The NRDC reported that the steamship exemption was spearheaded by the cruise line industry that lobbied to convince Congress to weaken the program (Kassel, 2012a; Kassel, 2012b). Ultimately, steamships were granted an exemption until 2020 (Kassel, 2010c).

The result of this case study: it is clear that initially the U.S. took the role of the lead state. ECAs were a U.S. idea that was introduced to the IMO via a U.S. proposal. By the time the ECAs were implemented, the U.S. took the role of a blocking state, pushing for the exemption of steamships from ECA regulations. This served to weaken the original proposal. Despite being a member of the U.S. delegation to the IMO, the NRDC was unable to influence the decision to include steamships in ECA regulation.

Case Five: World Bank And Coal Power Plants

In June 2013, President Obama unveiled his Climate Action Plan, a road map to cut carbon pollution in America, prepare the United States for the impacts of climate change and lead international efforts to combat global climate change and prepare for its impacts (Executive Office of the President, 2013, 5). This historic announcement left no doubt that the United States intended to take the lead role internationally. The plan also included the end to U.S. government support for new coal plants overseas (Executive Office of the President, 2013, 20); U.S. public credit agencies such as the Export-Import Bank of the United States (Ex-Im Bank) halted funding immediately. (The Ex-Im Bank assists in financing the export of U.S. goods and services to international markets) (Ex-Im Bank, About/Who We Are, 2013). The Climate Action Plan also outlined that the U.S. would "work actively to secure the agreement of other countries and the multilateral development banks to adopt similar policies as soon as possible" (Executive Office of the President, 2013, 20). The agreement from one multilateral development bank (MDB), the World Bank came quickly. By July 2013, the World Bank stated that it would support interventions that reduce GHG emissions associated with coal-combustion plants and that it would only provide financial support for a coal power plant project in rare circumstances (World Bank Group, 2013, 25). By November 20, 2013, the U.K. government issued a press release announcing,

> The U.K. will join the United States in agreeing to end support for public financing of new coal-fired power plants overseas, except in rare circumstances in which the poorest countries have no feasible alternative. The two governments will work together to secure the support of other countries and Multilateral Development Banks to adopt similar policies. (Department of Energy and Climate Change, 2013)

The evidence in this case study suggests that the NRDC may have had some influence on U.S. foreign policy behavior, albeit a limited one. The NRDC has actively campaigned to shut down existing coal power plants domestically and to halt the development of any new coal power plants in the US and abroad. Their 1986 victory of the "passage of legislation requiring the U.S. government to set up an 'early warning' system to track environmentally harmful multilateral bank projects" (NRDC, 2012d, About/Victories Archive) in part addressed the continuing financing of coal energy abroad. Since 2006, the NRDC has released several policy papers about GHG emissions from coal and their contribution to climate change (NRDC, Global Warming/Coal in a Changing Climate, 2012e). In 2010, the NRDC submitted detailed recommendations to the World Bank and the U.S. Government on developing an energy sector strategy which included the phase-out of high-GHG emitting fossil fuel lending in all client countries by 2015 (Schmidt, 2010). Notwithstanding the above, the NRDC has not claimed Obama's Climate Action Plan and the decision to stop funding coal power projects as their own victory. NRDC communication about MDBs and coal power projects simply applauds the steps taken by the U.S. government and MDBs to tackle climate change (Beinecke, 2013; Schmidt 2013a; Schmidt 2013b; Schmidt 2013c).

The result of this case study: the U.S. clearly took the role of a lead state. The U.S. explicitly stated its intended actions and foreign policy within the Climate Action Plan. NRDC communications regarding coal power plants, policy advice on climate change to the World Bank and the U.S. government (in advance of the release of the Climate Action Plan) suggests that the NRDC was able to influence the U.S. government to some extent.

Discussion

Academic literature provides some insight into how environmental interest groups influence state behavior. Bøås (2001, 182-183) suggests, NGOs cannot dictate terms to anyone; rather, an NGO such as the NRDC can only attempt to influence various branches of governments and thereby international organizations. Bøås suggests that environmental interest groups influence U.S. foreign policy by " linking different policy levels— local to the international, the national to the international and the national to the local, and so on" (2001,183). As subjects of municipal law, interest groups such as the NRDC must work by linking different policy levels if their objective is to influence state behaviour in the foreign policy environment. U.S. Public Law 99-500, Oct. 18, 1986 (legislation that the NRDC drafted) provides NGOs in the U.S. with the means to link different policy levels. In addition to the infamous 'early warning system', this legislation requires that the Treasury Department to compile and make available, "a list of projects that may adversely affect the environment to interested members of the public semi-annually" (U.S. Public Law 99-500, Oct. 18, 1986, 235). The release of this list provides civil society organizations a link from local to national, national to international level. In the fifth case study examined in this paper, despite the lack of hard evidence linking the NRDC to the U.S. decision to stop funding coal power plants in developing countries, it can be assumed that the NRDC did exert some influence to force institutional change. Recall that U.S. Public Law 99-500 provides NGOs with a list of funding requests by MDBs for coal power plants abroad six months in advance and regular access to U.S. decision makers at monthly meetings to review controversial oversea funding requests. This empowers the NRDC with the competency to voice their objections and views to U.S. decision makers regularly. The decision to stop funding overseas coal power plant projects was in alignment with NRDC priorities and historical policy recommendations and campaigns. Aufderheide and Rich (1988, 308) discuss in detail the strategy an environmental interest group can take to force institutional change: "U.S. environmental organizations understood early on that the multilateral development banks would never take their suggestions for environmental reform seriously [...] So they directed their attention to the major donor nations, on which the development banks depend for their funds". Aufderheide and Rich (1988, 308) rightly conclude that how funds are appropriated to MDBs is a source of great leverage for U.S. environmental organizations. Bøås suggests that because this leverage cannot be used directly, that "the NGOs' main path to influence is therefore to press their governments to express certain positions through the EDs[1]" (2001, 182). Nelson (2012, 19) offers a slightly different path of influence suggesting that because funds to MDBs are appropriated annually, withholding funding from an MDB or attaching stipulations can influence policy. As Porter and Brown (1996, 57) iterate, "primarily because of the importance of the U.S. Congress in approving funding for multilateral development banks, U.S. NGOs have been effective in forcing some changes in the lending of MDBs". Case study five (World Bank) strong suggests that the NRDC was able to influence how the U.S. government decides to appropriate funds and under which circumstances. International organizations like MDBs work on a weighted voting system, whereby countries that contribute more have a greater share of votes. Bøås' (2011, 191) observes that a strong link exists between the access NGOs have to U.S. decision makers, and the position the U.S. occupies in most MDBs as the major donor. The NGOs seek to influence the decision maker who in turn influences the appropriation of funds to an MDB.

Other international organizations such as the IMO and IWC operate under a different structure: one vote for each member state. The structural difference in the way an international organization operates may also be a consideration in a NGOs ability to influence a state to assume the lead role for a given issue. In case studies one and four in this paper, the NRDC was a member of the U.S. delegation to meetings at the IWC and IMO. The success or failure of the NRDC's objectives relied on their ability to influence the U.S. member to the NRDC's preferred position and subsequently the ability of the U.S. to corral the

---

[1] Executive Directors

support of other nations for a resolution to pass. In both case studies, the U.S. took a position that was not in alignment with NRDC objectives and priorities.

It can also be argued that the motivations for the U.S. to take a particular role in some cases have more to do with economics than concern for the environment. In the first case study with the IWC, the U.S. government contributed very little to the IWC annually. In 2011, the IWC only received $144,640 from the U.S. government (United States Department of State, 2011). If the size of this contribution gives an indication as to U.S. government inaction or indifference, this can explain why the U.S. government has not pressed for coordinated economic sanctions against Iceland; whaling, it seems, is not a priority for the US government. In the fourth case study that of the IMO, monetary concerns over the cost to retrofit steamships swayed the U.S. to change its role against its own original proposal. In the fifth case study, although the U.S. ended the funding of coal power plants, the Climate Action plan also called for American leadership and the export of American technology in natural gas exploration and gas plants to the international community (Executive Office of the President, 2013, 18-19).

Conclusion

Based on the five case studies, and the categorization of the results, my hypothesis is valid: the activities of the NRDC do not consistently push the U.S. government to act as a lead state in the foreign policy environment.

LEAD STATE	SUPPORTING STATE	SWING STATE	BLOCKING STATE
2	2	0	1

In only two of the five cases did the U.S. take a lead role in the foreign policy environment: the United Nations Convention on the Conservation and Management of High Seas Fisheries Resources in the North Pacific Ocean and the case study of the World Bank and coal-powered plants. Within these two case studies it cannot be conclusively stated that U.S. leadership was linked solely to NRDC influence.

For scholars and students, it is a useful exercise to examine and suggest how interests groups can influence a state's foreign policy behaviour because it provides an intimate understanding on how the political process works in a given country. The United States is a complex country that has complex bilateral and multilateral relationships. The examination of this environmental interest group's attempts to influence U.S. foreign policy behavior sheds some light on how civil society works to have their voices heard.

BIBLIOGRAPHY

Aufderheide, Pat and Bruce Rich. 1988. Environmental Reform and the Multilateral Banks. *World Policy Journal* **5**(2): 301-321

Beinecke, Frances. 2013, June, 25. Obama's Climate Action Plan Will Protect Our Health and Our Communities. [Switchboard: National Resources Defense Council Staff Blog]. <http://switchboard.nrdc.org/blogs/fbeinecke/obamas_climate_actio n_plan_wil.html>(2013, October 31).

Bøås, Morten, "Multilateral Development Banks, Environmental Impact Assessments, and Nongovernmental Organizations in U.S. Foreign Policy" in Paul G. Harris, ed., *The Environment, International Relations, and U.S. Foreign Policy*, Washington: Georgetown University Press, 2001, pp.178-196.

Department of Energy and Climate Change. 2013, November 20. UK urges the world to prepare for action on climate change and puts brakes on coal fired power plants.
≤https://www.gov.uk/government/news/uk-urges-the-world-to-prepare-for-action-on-climate-change-and-puts-brakes-on-coal-fired-power-plants> (2013, November 25).

Executive Office of the President. 2013. The President's Climate Action Plan. Washington: The White House
<http://www.whitehouse.gov/sites/default/files/image/president27sclimateactionplan.pdf>

Export-Import Bank (Ex-IM Bank) of the United States. 2013. About/Who We Are <http://www.exim.gov/about/whoweare/> (2013, November 25).

International Whaling Commission (IWC). 2012. Commercial Whaling. <http://iwc.int/commercial> (2013, November 24)

Kassel, Rich. 2010a, March 18. US/Canadian Proposal for Cleaner Ships Enters Final Stage Next Week. [Switchboard: National Resources Defense Council Staff Blog].
<http://switchboard.nrdc.org/blogs/rkassel/imo_alert_us_proposal_to_exemp.html > (2013, November 7).

Kassel, Rich. 2010b, September 24. IMO Alert: Proposal to Exempt Steamships Needs to be Changed. [Switchboard: National Resources Defense Council Staff Blog].
<http://switchboard.nrdc.org/blogs/rkassel/uscnadian_proposal_for_cleane.html> (2013, November 7).

Kassel, Rich. 2010c, October 5. IMO News: Steamships to be exempted from the North American Emission Control Area until 2020. [Switchboard: National Resources Defense Council Staff Blog]. <http://switchboard.nrdc.org/blogs/rkassel/us_exempts_steamships_from_its.html > (2013, November 7).

Kassel, Rich. 2012a, June 20. House vote today could cost up to 31,000 lives per year. [Switchboard: National Resources Defense Council Staff Blog]. <http://switchboard.nrdc.org/blogs/rkassel/house_vote_today_could_cost_up_1.html> (2013, November 7).

Kassel, Rich. 2012b, August 1. North American Emission Control Area goes into effect today- Important step forward for cleaner ships [Switchboard: National Resources Defense Council Staff Blog]. <http://switchboard.nrdc.org/blogs/rkassel/north_american_emission_contro.html> (2013, November 7).

Kiekow, Taryn. 2010, December 21. Groups Work to Stop Iceland's Illegal Whaling. [Switchboard: National Resources Defense Council Staff Blog]. <http://switchboard.nrdc.org/blogs/tkiekow/groups_work_to_stop_icelands_i.html> (2013, November 25).

Kiekow, Tary. 2011, September 15. U.S. Censures Iceland for Killing Whales. [Switchboard: National Resources Defense Council Staff Blog]. <http://switchboard.nrdc.org/blogs/tkiekow/us_censures_iceland_for_killing.html> (2013, October 31).

Kiekow, Taryn. 2013 June 19. Sad but true: Iceland has resumed hunting fin whales. [Switchboard: National Resources Defense Council Staff Blog]. <http://switchboard.nrdc.org/blogs/tkiekow/sad_but_true_iceland_has_resum.html> (2013, November 25).

Lehner, Peter. 2011, October 27. Global Phase-out of Lead in Gasoline
     Succeeds: Major Victory for Kid's Health. [Switchboard: National
     Resources Defense Council Staff Blog].
     <http://switchboard.nrdc.org/blogs/plehner/global_phase-
     out_of_lead_in_ga.html> (2013, November 25)

Locke, Gary. 2011, July 19. The Pelly Amendment to the Fishermen's
     Protective Act of 1967, 22 U.S.c. § 1978 [Official Letter to
     President]
     <http://www.noaanews.noaa.gov/stories2011/pdfs/pellygrantsignedl
     etter_final.pdf> (2013, November 25).

Mahant, Edelgard. Post-materialism and Foreign Policy. Diffusion and
     Evolution. Paper presented to the annual convention of the
     International Political Science Association, April 3-6, 2013, San
     Francisco.

Maroney, Katie. nrdcinfo@nrdc.org 2013, November 1. Stop whaling
     campaign [Personal email]. (2013, November 25).

National Resources Defense Council (NRDC). 2007, February 1.
     Protecting Ocean Habitat from Bottom Trawling.
     <www.nrdc.org/water/oceans/ftrawling.asp> (2013, October 31).

National Resources Defense Council (NRDC). 2010, April 22. Proposal
     to Legalize Commercial Whale Hunting Released.
     <http://www.nrdc.org/media/2010/100422b.asp> (2013, November
     25).

National Resources Defense Council (NRDC). 2011. Annual Report.
     <http://www.nrdc.org/about/annual/nrdc_annual_report2011.pdf>
     (2013, October 28).

National Resources Defense Council (NRDC). 2012a. About.
     http://www.nrdc.org/about/.
     (2013, October 8).

National Resources Defense Council (NRDC). 2012b. About NRDC: Who We Are <http://www.nrdc.org/about/who_we_are.asp> (2013, November 17).

National Resources Defense Council (NRDC). 2012c. About NRDC: Mission Statement <http://www.nrdc.org/about/mission.asp> (2013, November 18).

National Resources Defense Council (NRDC). 2012d. About NRDC: Victories Archive <http://www.nrdc.org/about/victories-archive.asp> (2013, November 18).

National Resources Defense Council (NRDC). 2012e. Global Warming: Coal in a Changing Climate <http://www.nrdc.org/globalwarming/coal/contents.asp> (2013, November 18).

Nelson, Rebecca M. 18 April, 2012. Multilateral Development Banks: Overview and Issues for Congress. Washington: Congressional Research Service. http://www.fas.org/sgp/crs/row/R41170.pdf

Obama, Barack. 2011, September 15.Memorandum regarding Pelly Certification and Icelandic Whaling <www.whitehouse.gov/the-press-office/2011/09/15/memorandum-regarding-pelly-certification-and-icelandic-whaling >(2013, October 31).

Porter, Gareth and Janet Welsh Brown. 1996. *Global Environmental Politics,* 2nd ed. Boulder: Westview Press.

Schmidt, Jake. 2010, September 14. It's time for the World Bank to marshal all of its energy resources to address climate change. [Switchboard: National Resources Defense Council Staff Blog]. <http://switchboard.nrdc.org/blogs/jschmidt/world_bank_energy_str ategy.html> (2013, October 20).

Schmidt, Jake. 2013a, April 3. Time for the World Bank to stop funding climate change: More fossil fuel funding isn't the answer. [Switchboard: National Resources Defense Council Staff Blog]. <http://switchboard.nrdc.org/blogs/jschmidt/time_for_the_world_ba nk_to_sto.html> (2013, October 20).

Schmidt, Jake. 2013b, July 18. World Bank to Stop Funding Coal Projects. [Switchboard: National Resources Defense Council Staff Blog]. <http://switchboard.nrdc.org/blogs/jschmidt/world_bank_to_stop_f unding_coa.html>(2013, October 20).

Schmidt, Jake. 2013c, July 18. Treasury Department to Stop Supporting U.S. Funding for Overseas Coal Projects. [Switchboard: National Resources Defense Council Staff Blog]. <http://switchboard.nrdc.org/blogs/jschmidt/treasury_department_to _stop_su.html>(2013, October 31).

U.S. Department of State. 2009, February 27. U.S. Opposes Iceland's Decision To Establish Large Commercial Whaling Quota. <www.state.gov/r/pa/prs/ps/2009/02/11874.htm> (2013, October 31).

United States Department of State. 2011. United States Department of State Sixtieth Annual Report –United States Contributions to International Organizations Report to Congress for Fiscal Year 2011. <www.state.gov/documents/organization/198906.pdf> (2013, October 31).

United States Environmental Protection Agency. 2008. International Maritime Organization Adopts Program to Control Air Emissions from Oceangoing Vessels. <http://epa.gov/otaq/regs/nonroad/marine/ci/420f08033.pdf≥

United Nations Department of Economic and Social Affairs. 2013. Introduction to ECOSOC Consultative Status. <http://esango.un.org/paperless/Web?page=static&content=intro> (2013, November 25).

U.S. Public Law 99-500.United States Statutes At Large, Volume 100, 99th Congress, 2nd Session, 18 October, 1986.

World Bank Group. 2013. Toward a Sustainable Energy Future for All: Directin for the World Bank Group's Energy Sector. <http://www.worldbank.org/content/dam/Worldbank/document/SD N/energy-secm2013-0281-2.pdf> (2013, November 25).

Willets, Peter. 1996. Consultative Status for NGOs at the UN. "The Conscience of the World". The Influence of Non-Governmental Organisations in the UN System. <http://www.staff.city.ac.uk/p.willetts/NGOS/CONSSTAT.HTM> (2013, November 25)

2. INTEREST GROUPS AND FOREIGN POLICY

A TWO LEVEL GAME ANALYSIS OF THE KEYSTONE XL
PIPELINE APPROVAL DELAY
By: Daniel Bodistean

A great point of contention between normally amicable trade partners has been brewing over what is now a five year period. With a long history of trade, dating back centuries, but more recently entrenched and liberalised with the NAFTA agreement, the USA and Canada are said to be the world's largest bilateral trading partners (excluding the EU taken as a whole). Although the relationship has faced challenges over the decades, few have been as contentious as the approval of the Keystone XL project. The Keystone XL pipeline project is the extended version of the original Keystone pipeline. The Keystone project was a 3,000 kilometer pipeline intended to carry heavy crude from the large producing Alberta to Illinois. This project was expanded by TransCanada, the company responsible, to the Keystone XL pipeline in 2008 representing a new 3,200 kilometer trajectory from Alberta to the oil refineries of Texas (<u>Maclean's 2012</u>).

The approval of this pipeline is complicated by the fact that the Canadian government sees it as vital to Canada's long term economic goals, whilst it possesses fewer economic incentives for the USA[2]. Moreover, it is further complicated by the fact that the pipeline requires approval from the American State

---

[2] Putnam predicts the difficulties caused by this in his two-level game analysis, stating "All-purpose support for international agreements is probably greater in smaller, more dependent countries with more open economies, as compared to more self-sufficient countries, like the United States... Ceteris paribus, more self-sufficient states with smaller win-sets should make fewer international agreements and drive harder bargains in those that they do make" (1988)

Department, effectively giving the American President a veto. It also seems to be a top priority for the Canadian government in their interactions with their American counterparts, as proved by numerous trips and personal correspondences regarding the issue.

In order to analyse the delay of the pipeline from a foreign policy perspective a two level analysis, as proposed by Putnam in his 1988 article[3], is particularly adept for this case. The intense local group lobby at the domestic level (level II) in the United States is often cited as the explanation for the delay of approval at the higher international level (level I). The hypothesis proposed is that level II actions taken by interests groups are in fact a plausible explanatory variable for the delay of approval for the Keystone XL pipeline in the USA.

Research Design

The explicative (independent) variable in this analysis is the involvement of various domestic groups in the issue. The subsequent reaction of the US administration (level I) negotiator will be said to be the response (dependant) variable. The objective of this paper is to seek a connection between the posturing and involvement of domestic groups and the delay of the infrastructure project. The analysis will hinge on the construction of the position of players along the maximisation continuum proposed by Putnam[4]. The movement along this continuum will be analysed for the possibility of win sets, paying attention to the movement of the American government's position which may have been caused by Level II pressure.

---

[3] *Diplomacy and Domestic Politics: the logic of Two-level game*(1988)
[4] On one side the maximum possible Canadian position, while the maximum possible American position will be assigned to the other side.

Despite the appropriateness of a game-theory analysis of the approval, this situation differs from the traditional example used by Putnam. The negotiations example used by Putnam implies a sit-down negotiation between the two parties, which does not exist in this case. This creates a situation of prolonged interaction between the two parties, but one which is still applicable because the two governments still interact and negotiate on the issue, but in a more ad hoc manner. Because of this prolonged interaction and for the sake of simplicity, the study of the movements along the continuum is split into four different time periods. The research moves in chronological order, beginning with the period February 2005- July 2008, followed by July 2008- July 2011, August 2011- January 18 2012 and finally ending with the period Jan 18, 2012- Sept. 2013. The periods were chosen because they mark significant movements of the players in their positions. Due to the uneven progression of the project, the periods are not of equal time increments, but this should not hinder analysis of the shifts of the players on the continuum and the possible causes of those shifts.

In order to render the analysis more parsimonious, the level I position of the Canadian federal Government, the Government of the Province of Alberta and TransCanada corporation will be merged together to represent one unified position on the issue[5]. This unified position will be taken as an exogenous variable for the sake of simplicity[6], and will not be

---

[5] This position will be said to be the foreign policy of Canada. Although such an assumption would strain credulity of the model under normal situations, it is rather simple to make in this case, due to the lockstep movement of the three actors in all instances related to Keystone project.

[6] A further analysis could be done on the construction of the Canadian position, but this is beyond the purview of this research. The effect of interest groups on

analysed as the construction of the American position will be.

As a result of the politicisation of this project, when referring to domestic groups, the paper goes beyond traditional foreign policy groups and takes into account the various interest groups that have become involved with the project. These include the environmental lobby groups, the Canadian oil production companies, trade advocacy groups and various non-traditional groups that have also chimed in on the issue.

Furthermore, due to the hyper politicisation of the issue, the Keystone XL project has recently been one of the most covered business stories in media in Canada. As previously mentioned, the issue is of particular importance to Canada; as a result there is a glut of articles being written north of the border, by Canadian publications of all types (from *Maclean's* to The *Globe and Mail*). South of the border, the issue has been gaining traction too, with various articles in publications such as *Forbes* and *The New York Times* among many others. Due to the ongoing nature of the issue, insider information is scarce, meaning that the majority of the data used originates from media rather than scholarly articles.

The theory proposed by Putnam in 1988 suggests that central decision makers cannot ignore either one of the two levels of the game. The politicisation of the Keystone and Keystone XL project midway through its approval provides us with a great opportunity to probe this thesis, by testing the effects of domestic politics on the "level I game" (i.e. the foreign policy) of the Obama administration. In the case of the American level II analysis of the delay, it will mostly hinge on the dissenting groups, which do not

---

The Canadian position is more difficult to map because a large part of it is backroom lobbying done by oil companies, creating difficulties in measure.

include the Republican Party (a supporter of the XL project). This in effect removes the possibility of level II institutional risk for President Obama, despite a great role of the review being played by the State and Federal governmental bodies (Maclean's 2012).

The Era of level I politicking

The time period between February 2005 and July 2008 may be called an "era of level I politicking", notably because during this period level II actions are largely absent. When level II action does occur, it receives little attention and has no noticeable bearing on the win sets of the administration. Public action against the Keystone Pipeline was largely absent from the debate until the latter part of 2008. This may have been due to the fact that the decision was still far away, which meant that both pro and contra parties could not create expectations of whether approval would be given or not.

During the period of February 2005 to September 2007, TransCanada proposed its original Keystone Pipeline project and was given approval by the Canadian National Energy Board (Canada.com 2007). A few months later, in March 2008, the Keystone Pipeline received the approval of the State Department and faced no veto from the American President (TransCanada 2008). The larger Keystone XL Pipeline was proposed in July 2008. The continuum representing the position of the two parties is constructed in Figure 1 below.

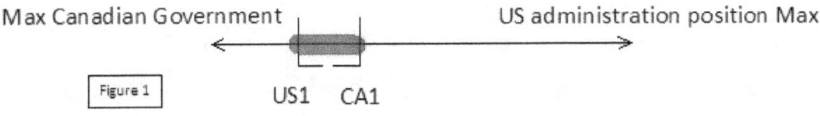

The positions of both the Canadian and American governments allowed for the Keystone Pipeline to be approved, meaning a possible win sets could have been reached. The distance between US1 and CA1 are in this case the possible win solutions, which is marked by the bolded area between the two. The approval of the larger Keystone XL Pipeline looks negotiable and feasible based on the previous interaction, which yielded a rather easy approval of the initial Keystone Pipeline. It would seem reasonable that no issue would arise since the pipeline carrying crude from Alberta was approved earlier. Because of the lack of big level II involvement in this period, we can deduce that this is in all likelihood the default level I position the two countries are willing to assume. It should also be noted that the US is more willing to compromise in this case than Canada, which has a fixed position, notably that of a full approval of the pipeline.

An all but certain approval

During the period of July 2008 to July 2011, the approval of the Keystone XL Pipeline seemed all but certain. In March 2010, The Natural Resources Defense Council, which is a non-profit from New York, published a damning report on the pipeline (Say No to Tar Sands Pipeline: Proposed Keystone XL Project Would Deliver Dirty Fuel at a High Cost). This is the first case of Level II interaction that received media attention, but it does not seem to have affected the approval process. Despite the report, the State Department released a draft Environmental Impact Statement, which claimed that the pipeline would have limited adverse impact on the environment in April 2010 (TransCanada 2013). This report was criticised by the EPA in July (Downstream Today 2010), indicating a certain level of internal discord, but which once again did not seem to cause a significant hindrance to the approval of the pipeline. This lack of impact was observed again in October 2010 when Hillary Clinton, the Secretary of State at the time, stated that she was "inclined to approve" the project (<u>Maclean's</u> 2012). The movements of the two players may be noted in Figure 2.

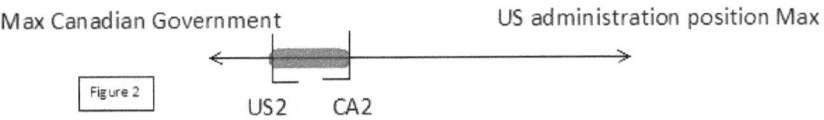

Max Canadian Government   US administration position Max

Figure 2

US2   CA2

In constructing the continuum for this time period, Canada's position remained the same, resulting from the fact that its position is an exogenous variable factor and that there was no change in its position. In essence, Canada still sought the same deal as before, namely having the pipeline approved in its entirety without compromise. The US position moved to the left, towards the Canadian maximum, creating a bigger space for win sets. This is due to the fact that little had changed from the previous actions of the US government, namely the Keystone Pipeline is still approved, but the Secretary of State showed signs of her being likely to approve the XL pipeline. The few reports and articles published against the pipeline do not seem to have affected the US government's position in this time period.

The Level II effect

In August 2011 the State Department released its final Environmental Impact Statement, concluding that there would be no long term adverse effects if the pipeline would be approved. Protests against the pipeline erupted outside the White House and actress Daryl Hannah along with 500 people staged a protest outside the White House. A total of 100 people were arrested after refusing to move from their place, including Hannah (Huffington Post 2011). The governor of Nebraska also asked President Obama to deny approval of the pipeline because the current route would put sensitive ecological zones in danger in that state. The governor changed his position in November when TransCanada proposed a new route, and the Nebraska legislator passed a bill approving the pipeline (CBC 2011). In September, Archbishop Desmond Tutu, the Dalai Lama and seven other Nobel Peace Prize laureates wrote to President Obama urging him to reject the pipeline (CBC 2011).

Public opposition intensified in early November 2011, with an estimated 10,000 protestors in front of the White House. They attracted a lot of media attention (Maclean's 2012). In December 2011, in order to pass a payroll bill, President Obama signed a bill that included a clause that would set the deadline for a decision on the pipeline by Feb. 21, 2012. This is an interesting case of the Canadians trying to exploit a heterogeneous US public opinion to their advantage, trying to use parties that support their plan (specifically the Republican Party), in order to put pressure on the American administration. Putnam predicts such a situation by stating that in cases of heterogeneous public opinion the "Level I negotiator may find silent allies at his opponent's domestic table" (Putnam 1988).

On January 18, 2012, the State Department rejected the pipeline, though with a lengthy explanation by President Obama. Normally this would signal an end to the negotiations, but President Obama stated that TransCanada could apply again because the rejection was due to the time constraints imposed on him and not because of the merits or lack thereof of the pipeline (Maclean's 2012). This is possible because of the lack of traditional sit down negotiations, envisaged by Putnam in his game theory analysis. The new continuum for the period between August 2011 and January 2012 may be seen in Figure 3.

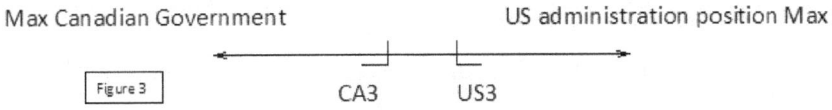

Max Canadian Government | US administration position Max

Figure 3   CA3   US3

The US position clearly moved towards the right, which is its own maximum. The US moved from a position where it was very likely to approve the pipeline to one where it was less likely to do so. It seems that the lobbying and protests at level II had an impact on the level I position of the government. The position of TransCanada and the Canadian Government moved slightly towards the US maximum because of their willingness to change the trajectory of the pipeline to one more convenient for the US. The win set however is still non-existent, as the two positions do not create an area of possible intersection. This can be explained by the basic fact that the pipeline was rejected.

Canadian Government Action

The period between January 2012 and September 2013 is marked by various actions taken by the Canadians. In February 2012, TransCanada separated the project in two, proceeding with construction of the part that does not cross the border, which therefore does not need State Department approval. The president publicly supported the American leg of the pipeline, even going so far as saying that he will expedite the permission (TransCanada 2013). In May 2012, TransCanada submitted an application to the US government for approval of the part of the project that would cross the border. The proposal, which remains the same until today, includes a new route for Nebraska avoiding the sensitive Sandhills which were a point of contention for the Governor of that state (TransCanada 2013). Premier Redford of Alberta travelled to Washington to lobby for Keystone XL in April of 2013. She met with congress members and promoted Canada's environmental credentials, including Alberta's carbon tax (CBC 2013). This is an interesting case of what Putnam described in the latter part of his article as reverberation. In essence premier Redford was attempting to "relax domestic constraints that might otherwise prevent the administration from cooperating with their governments" (Putnam 1988), in order to put pressure for approval and move the position of the American administration on the continuum.

In September of the same year, sources said that the Canadian PM offered President Obama a possibility of a climate deal, in order to secure approval of the Keystone XL pipeline (CBC 2013). This is an example of the Canadian government moving towards the American position in order to open up possible win-sets. Having seen that approval could not be taken for granted; the Canadian government became more flexible in its own position. The Canadian Government appears to be consciously acting on a rational choice model, attempting to open up win-sets by moving its own position along the spectrum and putting pressure on the administration by changing level II opinion about Canada and the project. The movements may be observed in Figure 4.

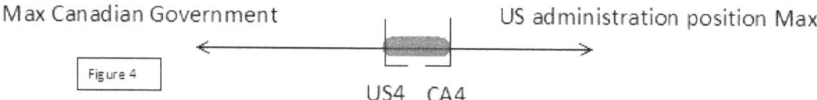

Max Canadian Government   US administration position Max

Figure 4

US4   CA4

The new positions assumed by the two parties created a possibility of win-sets because almost all sources believe that the project will be approved in the end. Interestingly, Canada started out in a position quite advantageous for itself, but because of movements in the American position, it had to modify its position and move closer towards the goals of the US.

Conclusion

In conclusion, it seems that in the case of the Keystone XL Pipeline, level II mobilisation moved a project from a state of imminent approval, as stated by Secretary Clinton, to a situation where the project was denied. The hypothesis that level II actions taken by interests groups are in fact a plausible explanatory variable on the level I actions, holds true to a certain degree. However, issues arise regarding the model when looking at statistics of public opinion in the USA regarding the pipeline. According to a survey done by Harris Interactive, on behalf of the American Petroleum Institute 77% of Americans think the pipeline will strengthen national security and 81% think it will strengthen the USA's energy security. A similar pattern can be observed even when taking into account partisanship, with 83% of Republicans, 69% of Independents, 63% of Democrats supporting the construction of the project (Industry Today 2013).With public opinion being so one-sided, the interest of the level II actors maybe be said to be pro the pipeline rather than against it.

The hypothesis seems conceivable, but in order to better account for the public opinion data, future research will require a more refined model to explain the Level II impact. The model used in this research assumes level II positioning as being equally weighted among individual citizens. Holding this assumption seems to disprove the hypothesis proposed at the beginning, as public opinion seems to support the project, rather than condemn it. A model which assigns differently weighted importance to the various groups within Level II might have more explanatory power. In this model the importance of groups may have to differ across time, and be subject to Level I politics, including being sensitive to administration changes[7]. Such a model might also be used to probe the thesis proposed by Richard Levick of *Forbes*, who states that approval for the pipeline was voiced by activists on social media, who used the "amplifying" effect of social media in order to create more stir than is displayed by the actual public support that the pipeline seems to enjoy.

BIBLIOGRAPHY

Avok, Michalel (2011) Nebraska governor Dave Heineman signed into law on Tuesday bills to reroute the Keystone XL pipeline away from the ecologically sensitive Sandhills region. Reuters. Available at: http://www.reuters.com/article/2011/11/22/us-oil-pipeline-nebraska-idUSTRE7AL1M120111122. Accessed November 7.

Conca, James (2013) What Is Wrong With The Keystone XL Pipeline? Forbes. Available at: http://www.forbes.com/sites/jamesconca/2013/08/25/what-is-wrong-with-the-keystone-xl-pipeline. Accessed October 8, 2013.

Gerken, James (2011) Daryl Hannah Arrested At Keystone XL Pipeline Protest. Huffington Post. Available at: http://www.huffingtonpost.com/2011/08/30/daryl-hannah-arrested-keystone-protest_n_942072.html. Accessed November 9.

Graves, Lucia (2011) State Department Moves Forward On Construction Of Keystone XL Oil Pipeline. Huffington Post. Available at : http://www.huffingtonpost.com/2011/08/26/state-department-keystone-xl-oil-pipeline_n_938138.html. Accessed November 6.

---

[7] It should be noted that the United States faced an administration change in 2009, during the approval process of the pipeline. It is very well conceivable that the new Obama administration might be more swayed by different level II groups than the ones which greatly swayed the Bush administration.

Hagget, Scott (2008) TransCanada, Conoco to extend pipeline to U.S.
Gulf. Reuters. Available at:
http://www.reuters.com/article/2008/07/16/us-transcanada-
idUSWNAB091120080716. Accessed November 6.

Hall, Chris (2013)Analysis Harper offers Obama climate plan to win
Keystone approval. CBC. Available at:
http://www.cbc.ca/news/politics/harper-offers-obama-climate-
plan-to-win-keystone-approval-1.1701391.Accessed November
6.

Hovey, Art (2008) TransCanada Proposes Second Oil Pipeline. Lincoln
Journal-Star. Available at:
http://www.downstreamtoday.com/news/article.aspx?a_id=1133
6&AspxAutoDetectCookieSupport=1. Accessed October 8,
2013.

Industry Today (2013) KEYSTONE XL PIPELINE: A Pipeline to a
Better Tomorrow. Industry Today. Vol. 16,
No. 6. Available at:
http://industrytoday.com/article_view.asp?ArticleID=F417.
Accessed November 8.

Levick, Richard (2013) Infographics: Why TransCanada Is Losing The
Keystone Pipeline Debate. Forbes. Available at:
http://www.forbes.com/sites/richardlevick/2013/10/15/infographi
cs-why-transcanada-is-losing-the-keystone-pipeline-debate/2/ .
Accessed November 5.

Maclean's (2011) It's time for Canada to seek other friends besides the
U.S. Maclean's. Available at:
http://www2.macleans.ca/2011/11/21/it%E2%80%99s-time-for-
canada-to-seek-other-friends-besides-the-u-s/ . Accessed
November 6.

Ministry of Finance Canada (2013) Bilateral Relations: Canada-US Trade and Investment. Available at: http://actionplan.gc.ca/en/page/bbg-tpf/bilateral-relations-canada-us-trade-and-investment. Accessed October 9, 2013.

Natural Resource Defence Council (2010) Say No to Tar Sands Pipeline. Available at: http://www.nrdc.org/land/tarsandspipeline.asp. Accessed November 6.

Payton, Laura (2011) Nobel winners urge Keystone rejection. CBC. Available at: http://www.cbc.ca/news/politics/nobel-winners-urge-keystone-rejection-1.1083800 . Accessed November 4.

Perdomo and Vieira (2012) Keystone XL: a timeline. Maclean's. Available at: http://www2.macleans.ca/2012/01/18/keystone-xl-a-timeline/. Accessed November 5.

Putnam, Robert D. (1988) Diplomacy and Domestic Politics: The Logic of Two-Level Games. *International Organization* Vol. 42, No. 3 (Summer, 1988), pp. 427-460.

Savage, Luisa (2010) Hillary Clinton: "inclined to" okay Keystone XL pipeline. Maclean's. Available at: http://www2.macleans.ca/2010/10/20/hillary-clinton-inclined-to-okay-keystone-xl-pipeline/. Accessed November 5.

The Associated Press (2011) Nebraska governor tells Obama to deny Keystone permit. CBC. Available at: http://www.cbc.ca/news/canada/edmonton/nebraska-governor-tells-obama-to-deny-keystone-permit-1.993708. Accessed November 7.

The Canadian Press (2013) Alberta premier lobbying for Keystone XL
    pipeline in Washington. CBC.
    Available at: http://www.cbc.ca/news/canada/edmonton/alberta-
    premier-lobbying-for-keystone-xl-pipeline-in-washington-
    1.1391276.   Accessed November 6.

The Edmonton Journal (2007) NEB approves pipeline to U.S.
    Canada.com. Available at:
    http://www.canada.com/edmontonjournal/news/business/story.ht
    ml?id=9dccab68-4e21-4888-9c55-5a3de86100e8. Accessed
    November 8.

TransCanada (2008) Keystone Oil Pipeline receives Presidential Permit –
    Construction to begin in second
    quarter of 2008. Available at:
    http://www.transcanada.com/3036.html. Accessed November 6.

TransCanada (2013) About the Project. Available at:
    http://keystone-xl.com/about/the-project.
    Accessed October 8.

TransCanada (2013) Keystone XL Timeline. Available at:
    http://www.transcanada.com/social/responsibility/2011/keystone
    _xl/timeline/. Accessed November 5.

Uechi, Jenny (2013) Harper begs Obama for Keystone XL approval.
    Vancouver Observer. Available at:
    http://www.vancouverobserver.com/environment/harper-begs-
    obama-keystone-xl-approval . Accessed November 6.

Welsch, Edward (2010) EPA Calls for Further Study of Keystone XL.
    Downstream Today. Available at:
    http://www.downstreamtoday.com/news/article.aspx?a_id=2343
    4&AspxAutoDetectCookieSupport=1. Accessed November

3. EU ENLARGEMENT

WILL TURKEY BE INCLUDED?
By: Alexandra Pullano

Turkey's relationship with the European Union dates back to a relationship with the union's predecessor, the European Economic Community, which began in 1959, when Turkey first applied for membership. Turkey's membership was not accepted, however negotiations proceeded and an association agreement was established, titled the Ankara agreement, in 1963. The association agreement was written with the aim of creating a customs union between the two entities and provided for the possibility of membership, after the achievement of the customs union. This progress however, was sidelined during domestic upheaval in Turkey due to the military coups in the 1980's, which froze relations. As Turkey's domestic politics normalized, it began a process of aligning their policies with Europe and applied for membership in 1985. In 1987, the Union rejected this application, claiming Turkey was unprepared to hold the responsibilities of membership. After this rejection, Turkey continued its attempt to align its policies with Europe and achieved a customs union in 1996. However, in 1997, Turkey was left out of enlargement negotiations during the Luxembourg Conference, which led Turkey to freeze relations. Negotiations were restored and in 1999, a watershed moment was reached, when Turkey was granted member candidate status at the Helsinki conference. In 2004, the European Commission declared that Turkey had achieved the Copenhagen Criteria and negotiations for membership were opened in 2005. However, 18 out of 22 chapters of negotiations have been blocked. Thus, it is generally projected that Turkish membership, if it comes at all, will not happen for at least another ten to fifteen years.

This history with the European community makes Turkey one of the countries with the longest history of integration with the European Union. This fact begs the question why has the negotiations surrounding Turkish integration, been so controversial and long-winded, especially in comparison to other membership applications. This paper will attempt to answer this question by providing an analysis of the major policy decisions regarding Turkey's status with Europe, outlined in the previous paragraph. This paper presents the hypothesis that, negotiations with Turkey and the EU have been noticeably different when compared to negotiations with other states; due to identity politics which claim that Turkey is not a European country. In order to test this hypothesis, each event will be analyzed based on official European decision documents, statements made by European decision-makers, public opinion surveys and scholarly debate. These decisions will then be compared to decisions during other comparable membership applications. It is beyond the scope of the paper to define what Turkish and European identities entail, rather the paper will simply be providing an analysis of what these identities are perceived to be and how these perceptions have shaped negotiations. The aim of this paper is to place decisions in regards to Turkey in the political context of the time, in order to find the factors that influenced these decisions, beginning with the establishment of the Ankara agreement.

From the beginning, negotiations surrounding Turkey's integration with the economic community was characterised by a lack of enthusiasm from the member states and differential treatment, in comparison to other states seeking integration. The European Economic Community (EEC), meant for The Ankara

Agreement signed in 1963, to be modeled in the same vein as Greece's 1961 association agreement, however negotiations conducted with the two countries ended up being markedly different from each other (Tatham, 142). Firstly, the EEC indicated its divergent attitude towards Turkey in comparison to Greece, in the length of negotiations needed, to establish an agreement between the two parties. Negotiations with Greece and the community were less prolonged than the ones on the Ankara Agreement with Turkey (Mayer, 4). Both Turkey and Greece applied for membership in 1959; however Greece achieved association in 1961(Tatham, 28), while Turkey's agreement did not come until 1963. The length of negotiations is important in measuring the EEC's enthusiasm and motivation to accept a state into its fold. The fact that negotiations with Turkey took much longer than similar negotiations with Greece is indicative of the European Community's reservations towards Turkey, as it took longer to establish conditions which make the close association with Turkey agreeable to the European Community.

Additionally, internal European politics within the EEC also hindered the implementation of certain provisions in the Ankara agreement. The most contentious issue laid out in the Agreement was the issue of the free movement of peoples. The agreement states in article 12 that the EEC and Turkey had agreed to "be guided by Articles 48, 49 and 50 of the Treaty (which founded the EEC), establishing the Community for the purpose of progressively securing freedom of movement for workers between them." This clause clearly states that the EEC had agreed to provide for a free movement of workers between the community and Turkey under the same conditions that governed free movement of workers between existing members of the community. However, in contradiction to this statement, the EEC put in place provisions on freedom of movement with Turkey that were not added to similar agreements with countries such as Spain and Portugal (Mayer, 2). Moreover, Article 12 of the Ankara association never became a reality since veto points maintained by member states in the Council, meant that the freedom of movement was never established (Mayer, 5). Here, it is clear that Turkey's association engenders a division among the community over how far the association should extend. This indicates that the community was less open to provisions that would prompt a deeper integration rather than a superficial economic association.

The implementation of the Ankara agreement proceeded steadily until the shock of the Turkish military coup of 1980, which suspended Turkish-EEC integration. Prior to the coup Turkey had progressed to the second stage, the transitional stage, of the agreement and an additional protocol that aimed to establish the free movement of goods, services and people entered into force in 1973 (Serdaroğlu, 2013). With the military coup, this progress was reversed and the European trade union within the European parliament led a campaign that resulted in the suspension of the Ankara agreement on January 22, 1982 (Serdaroğlu, 2013). The suspension based on the military coup can be viewed as fair, since the coup and the establishment of a military dictatorship contradicted the goals of an open and free economy, inherent in the agreement and the goals of the community. However, its response to the military coup in Turkey was much harsher than its response to a similar coup in Greece around the same time.

While the Ankara agreement was completely suspended, the agreement with Greece continued to allow for tariff reductions (Tatham, 30). Moreover, the timeline of normalization and progression of negotiations were noticeably different between Turkey and Greece. Once Greece returned to democracy in 1974, they applied for membership negotiations, which the community agreed to open (Tatham, 31). From this decision, Greece entered into a pre-accession period and concluded membership negotiations on May 23, 1979. Membership was granted in an effort for the ECC to be seen as supporting the still-fragile democracies in the South of Europe (Tatham, 31). Moreover, Germany pushed for Greece's accession in fear that a rejection would have a negative impact on its NATO membership (Tatham, 31). Here, Greece was able to benefit from a member state's backing and member states perception that Greece, as a member of the continent, was entitled to European support.

Normalization with Turkey however, did not bring about any changes in the agreement already signed and did not lead to membership. Firstly, the community opposed any changes on financial protocol, such as refusing to approve the 4th Financial Protocol (Progress Report,1990), or free movement of workers, despite noticeable improvements in Turkey's domestic situation (Tatham, 144). What is more, like Greece, Turkey applied for membership in 1987 however, unlike Greece, a decision and membership did not arrive within the same year. The EEC's lack of enthusiasm for Turkey's membership was evidenced by the two and half years it took for it to prepare its opinion, which ultimately rejected the application (Tatham, 144). In addition, Spain and Portugal, countries who also recently returned to democracy, acceded to the community around the same time (Saatcioglu, 5), in an attempt to bring these countries "back into Europe" (Ruiz-Jimenez, 8). Clearly, the EEC did not feel that Turkey was included in the fragile democracies of the South of Europe that necessitated EEC aid to be reintegrated into Europe, in which the community felt they belonged. Turkey was unable to benefit from a member states backing and member states did not feel that Turkey was entitled to membership, as the community stated in regards to the accessions of Spain, Greece and Portugal. This discrepancy between otherwise similar situations emphasizes Turkey's perceived outsider status with the European community.

In the European Commission's decision in 1989, the commission based its official rejection of the application on political and economic shortcomings, yet the decision also added the community's ability to absorb Turkey as an additional criteria. In terms of economics the commission focused on structural problems, mainly Turkey's reliance on agriculture, which accounted for 50% of its workforce, along with macroeconomic imbalances, industrial protectionism and low social protections (Tatham, 145). Here, it is important to note that at the time of its accession Greece had similar dependence on agriculture and was far from problem free in economics (Tatham). Secondly, the commission expressed reservations on Turkey's political and democratic health. It maintained that while there have been developments, human rights and respect for minorities had not reached the level of democracy (Tatham, 146). These reservations were warranted as, at the time, Turkey did have work to do in terms of modernization of the economy and ensuring a democratic environment which was heavily influenced by the military. However, the commission in its 1989 decision also alluded to the fact that Turkey's ability to meet the economic and political criteria would not ensure its accession.

In paragraph six of the European Commission's decision, it stated that accession would hinge on the "EU's ability to absorb Turkey" (Saatcioglu, 5). The commission referred to it being a large country both in terms of geography and in population, to justify this assertion (Tatham, 145). With Turkey's growing population, upon accession it would be the second largest member of the union, and would be on track to become the largest country, surpassing Germany (Sklias, 198). Thus, Turkey would have proportionally a large influence and voting power if it were accepted into the Union. As a result, the Union was worried about being overwhelmed by Turkey's membership. This decision marked the first time the EU explicitly signaled that Turkey's membership issue was bigger than its domestic reform problems (Saatcioglu, 5). Here, the debate turned from whether Turkey was ready for membership, to whether the EU was ready for Turkey.

Additionally, the issue of Turkey and Cyprus began to enter into the debates about Turkey's membership. Turkey's continuing military presence in Cyprus was a major sticking point in negotiations. On numerous occasions, the EU stated that Turkish-EU relations could not be separated from the Cyprus question (Westering, 20). Thus, Turkey's rejection of removing its troops from the island country hindered the implementation of progression in negotiations. An important example is the delaying of the implementation of the customs union for a year and the blocking of the financial package by Greece (Westering, 104), due to objections based on the lack of progress in Cyprus negotiations (Tatham, 146). The European Union's treatment of its relations between Cyprus and Turkey bring up a number of discrepancies. Enthusiasm for the accession of Cyprus has been noticeably different than the attitude towards Turkey's accession. Just as the with the accession of Spain, Portugal and Greece, Cyprus had been deemed destined to join the European Union due to its undeniable European identity. In the European Commission's 1993 Opinion on Cyprus it declared:

Cyprus's geographical position, the deep-lying bonds which...have located the island at the very fount of European culture and civilization, the intensity of the European influence apparent in the values shared by the people of Cyprus and in the conduct of the cultural, political, economic and social life of its citizens, the wealth of its contacts of every kind with the Community, all these confer on Cyprus, beyond all doubt, its European identity and character, and confirm its vocation to belong to the Community (Tatham, 131).

In contrast, Turkey has never received such a ringing endorsement and assurance of its inevitable and inherent membership in the community, rather even when Turkey's eventual membership has been treated positively, it is only spoken about in the context of a security and strategic choice (Avci, 94). The European Union's clear support of Greek Cyprus desires, over those of Turkey is a consistent obstacle for negotiations moving forward.

The Copenhagen Decision of 1993, further aggravated tensions between Turkey and the EU since ex- communist regimes, along with Cyprus, were guaranteed accession in the near future, while Turkey's status did not progress. The decision explicitly stated "the associated countries in Central and Eastern Europe that so desire *shall* become EU members" and added that "the future cooperation with the associated countries shall be geared to the objective of *membership*" (Copenhagen, June 21-22 1993, emphasis added). This statement provided no ambiguities and assured the ex-communist countries membership. In contrast, the Copenhagen decision declared, in regards to Turkey, that its immediate objective was not accession but the furthering of economic relations (Saatcioglu, 6). The decision asks that the

Council ensure the effective implementation of all relevant documents "as far as it relates to the establishment of a *customs union*" (Copenhagen, June 21-22 1993, emphasis added), but did not allude to any negotiations in regards to accession in the near future.

It was particularly difficult for Turkey to watch the ex-Soviet states, which did not have the same level of association with the European community as Turkey, head to the "front of the line" for accession (Tatham, 120). Here, the European Union justified the eventual accession of former communist regimes, as a policy of "moral duty" and, echoing decisions for Greece, Portugal and Spain, to help them "return to Europe" (Saatcioglu, 6). The decision further declares that "its Member States pledge their support to this reform process. Peace and security in Europe depend on the success of those efforts" (Copenhagen, June 21-22 1992). Here, it is clear that accession in previous enlargement processes, have been used as a means to enact change. The union hoped that accession would bring the policies of these countries in line with the democratic and social values of the community and away from the communist or dictatorial regimes which characterised the nations before negotiations. This was seen as a means to stabilize Europe. In contrast, Turkey is expected to enact changes in its domestic situation before negotiations are opened. It is with this context that reference to the Europe as a project designed to create a union of nations with one shared common identity, becomes apparent. This is expressed by statements from Christian Democratic leaders in the EU, that declare the EU is a "civilizational project" (Avci, 94), which indicates that an important factor in membership for these groups is the adherence to a common "European culture". Following the 1997 decision, Wilfried Martens, a prominent Christian Democrat in the European Parliament stated "the EU is in the process of building a civilisation in which Turkey has no place" (The Economist, 1997). These groups often expressed their opposition on religious grounds, citing Turkey's majority Muslim population as being contrary to the perceived Judeo-Christian, European identity (Aydin, 180). The lack of endorsement of Turkey and the lack of support from the European Union, based on identity politics, signifies that, the perceived identity of a state is important to whether or not membership is afforded to them.

The Luxembourg decision of 1997, dealt a significant blow to Turkish- EU relations, as Turkey was left out of the group of countries that were being considered for membership. Cyprus along with ex- Soviet states were given pre-accession status, ahead of Turkey, leading Turkish officials to claim to be victims of discriminatory treatment from the EU (Tatham, 149). This was due to the fact that both Cyprus, and the ex-communist states that began accession negotiations at this time, could be said to have not fulfilled the Copenhagen criteria upon the opening of negotiations. For example, the Copenhagen criteria states that a country must "achieve institutional stability as a guarantee of democratic order … *before* accession negotiations are opened" (Westering, 113). However, in the case of Cyprus, not only did it not meet this stipulation when negotiations were opened, it did not achieve institutional stability upon accession. The island of Cyprus is divided between two governing authorities that of the Greek Cypriots and on the other side the Turkish Cypriots. The Greek- Cypriot government, which the EU officially recognizes, does not have de facto control over the entirety of the island, since they cannot step foot on part of the territory for which, on paper, it is responsible (Westering, 113). Moreover, the ex-communist regimes lagged economically in comparison to current member states, and had not fully achieved a free market economy (Saatcioglu, 7). Thus, it is evident that the European Union has been willing to overlook weaknesses in economics and domestic governance, when the member state in question has been perceived to undeniably be part of the European civilization.

Changing political tides within the European Union, especially in regards to Greece and Germany, led to a watershed moment in 1999, where the Helsinki decision formally accorded Turkey the status of EU candidate country. While the 1997 decision was heavily influenced by the identity politics of Christian Democrat governments and parties, a switch to progressive governments in Greece and Germany, engendered a more favourable perspective on Turkey's status within the Union. Up until this point, Greek governments had worked to veto Turkey's accession progress (Saatcioglu, 7), based on historical tensions and conflicts between the two countries (Keridis, 157). However, prior to the Helsinki decision, Theo Pangalos was replaced as foreign minister by George Papandreou, who was a progressive left wing politician and thus held a more moderate view toward relations with Turkey (Tatham, 150). Additionally, an earthquake that hit Greece and Turkey was instrumental in changing Greek public opinion in regards to Turkey. As a result of the earthquake, the countries provided mutual assistance in solidarity, which produced waves of support for Turkey (Tatham, 150). Therefore, with Greece projecting a favourable outlook on Turkey at this time, a persistent roadblock was eliminated in the lead up to the Helsinki decision.

Secondly, the election of a social-democratic government in Germany provided Turkey with an endorsement from a powerful member state. During the decisions in 1997, Germany was governed by the Christian Democratic leader Helmt Kohl, whose government was known to have negative attitudes towards Turkey and hold similar views to those expressed by Wilfried Martens (The Economist, 1997). Since Germany was the "big European power" (The Economist, 1997), this negative attitude from Kohl hindered Turkey's prospect. Thus, the change of government from a Christian Democratic party to a moderate social-democratic party under Gerhard Shroeder, was advantageous for Turkey in 1999. Gerhard Schroeder marked a profound change from Kohl's position, evidenced by his proposal to resolve the position of Turks in Germany, which had been precarious under the previous government (Tatham, 151). In the first half of 1999, Germany held the presidency of the EU which it used to create a draft proposal to reverse the Luxembourg Council's decision (Tatham, 151). Thus, with the support of the Greek and German governments, the Helsinki Council 1999 confirmed the accession process and Turkey's status as a candidate country.

While the Helsinki decision was the most supportive pronouncement of Turkey's eventual membership since the Ankara Agreement, it did not provide a specified timetable for accession. Thus, as seen in previous stages of Turkey's relationship with the European Community, the Helsinki declaration did not speed up Turkey's membership. It was not until 2002 that the European Union provided a decision on Turkey's progress. In this decision the Copenhagen Euro Council urged Turkey to address remaining shortcomings in regards to the Copenhagen Criteria and stipulated that negotiations would open in December of 2004, provided that all criteria had been met (Tatham, 152). However, the political climate that had been favourable to Turkey in 1999 was being reversed with the rise of right wing political figures. For example, French politician Valery Giscard D'Estaing declared at this time, that Turkey's entry into the EU would be "the end of Europe" because it was not a European country (Fsadni, 176). These sentiments were echoed by the European public in the wake of the 2001 attacks on the Twin Towers. With the emergence of a discourse on the 'War on Terror' and the Islamist attacks in Madrid and London, there has been a sentiment among the population linking Muslims and the potential for terrorism (Tzampiris, 68). Thus, Turkey's Muslim population, and its perceived Islamism, began to play a more explicit role in perceptions of its eligibility for membership.

While, the European Union's progress report in 2003, stated that Turkey had fulfilled the criteria sufficiently to allow the European Council to decide to open negotiations, (Tatham 152), debates regarding the desirability of a Turkish membership intensified. In the lead up to the Brussels summit which would decide on whether to open negotiations or not, statements from a number of European politicians provided evidence that identity factors were the main concern for many of the negotiators. This reflects the fact that, the debate is currently taking place as part of European identity crisis within a Europe that is becoming preoccupied more and more with its identity, borders and future (Fsadni,161 and Aydin, 171).German Chancellor, Angela Merkel led this opposition and lobbied EU heads of state for an inclusion of a reference to the idea of a "privileged partnership", stating that this partnership "would be more valuable than an underprivileged Turkish membership in the EU" (Saatcioglu, 14). Here it is important to note that it is assumed that even with Turkish accession, it would be "underprivileged" in the group rather than an equal. Merkel's position was accepted by Austrian Chancellor Wolfgang Schussel and France's Nicolas Sarkozy

(Saatcioglu, 14). Throughout the summit statements from politicians expressed concerns related to Islamophobia and a fear of immigration. For example, Dutch European Commissioner Frits Balkstein warned of the "Islamization of Europe", while Olli Rehn the then Enlargement Commissioner said he 'would seek a special provision to allow the EU to indefinitely close its borders to Turkish immigrants" (Saatcioglu, 14). Clearly, the debate at this time was increasingly in reference to Turkey's identity in relation to Europe, rather than if it has achieved the Copenhagen Criteria, indicating that Turkish accession hinges on its ability to be perceived by the Union as European.

The Brussels Summit of 2004 did declare that Turkey had met the provisions of the Copenhagen Criteria and thus had earned the ability to enter into membership negotiations, but not without extenuating conditions. Within this political context, the 2004 Brussels Council formulated exceptionally difficult terms which tied Turkey's membership to unprecedented conditions that had not been imposed on any previous EU candidate state (Saatcioglu, 15). Reflecting the fact that public opinion was easily stirred against migration (Sklias, 201), the EU declared that special arrangements could be considered regarding freedom of movement of persons by enacting a "permanent safeguard clause", which would give Turkey a "second-class status" (Saatcioglu, 15) in the Union, upon accession. Moreover, Merkel achieved her goal, a privileged partnership rather than membership would be considered in the continuing open-ended negotiations with Turkey (Saatcioglu, 15). Under these stipulations, negotiations began in 2005. However, the statement of this decision was far from reassuring and did not guarantee membership. The document stated:

These negotiations are an *open-ended process*, the outcome of which cannot be   guaranteed beforehand. While having full regard to all Copenhagen criteria, including the   absorption capacity of the Union, if Turkey is not in a position to assume in full all the   obligations of membership, it must be ensured that Turkey is fully anchored in the European structures through the strongest possible bond (Tataham, 154).

This statement marks the first time that the European Union has provided for a failure in the negotiation process. It seems contradictory since accession is meant to be the aim of talks, yet failure is not being ruled out (Tatham 154). This statement is quite different than the ones provided for the ex-soviet states and Cyprus, who were guaranteed membership from the outset of the negotiation process.

Moreover, the Union is expressing its reluctance toward Turkish accession by explicitly mentioning 'the absorption capacity' as a criterion for membership. Here the absorption capacity had been elevated to, and given as much force, as membership conditionality, rather than a simple consideration (Saatcioglu, 17), as it had been with previous candidate states. The decision further stated that "the EU's ability to maintain and deepen its own development in terms of policies and institutions, while pursuing an enlargement agenda" along with European citizen's support for enlargement would also be considered (Saatcioglu, 17). This statement can be seen as a direct result of the French and Dutch referendums which rejected the new European constitution, which scholars have said was a reaction of public discontent towards enlargement (Anvanitopoulos and Tzifakis, 2). A Eurobarometer survey in 2006 also found that satisfaction with the Union had dropped. Thus, being wary of this declining faith in the institution and its legitimacy, the Union is less willing to engage in policies that are not greatly supported by the public. Here, it is clear that growing "enlargement fatigue" and a public instinct to avoid the mental changes and discomfort that newcomers bring (Keridis, 155), are contributing to the decisions made when debating Turkish accession. While previous enlargements had been framed by the candidate countries ability to bare the responsibilities of membership, the EU has conditioned Turkey's membership on whether or not the EU is able to accept Turkey.

Thus, negotiations are currently largely at a standstill with many of the negotiation chapters being blocked, thus Turkey's future with the EU is unknown. As it now stands, 18 of the 22 chapters have been blocked. This is due in large part to the situation in Cyprus which remains a large roadblock in negotiations as neither side has been able to compromise. Thus, the suspension of 8 of the blocked chapters is due to Turkish reluctance to open its trade and ports to vessels from Cyprus (Tatham, 155). An agreement and negotiation on the Cyprus issue is essential to progression of Turkish accession in order to unblock these chapters and to lift the Cypriot veto against Turkish accession. However, Cyprus is not the only roadblock in the opening chapter negotiations. In 2008, France vetoed the opening of 5 chapters as they were considered to directly contribute to the prospect of Turkish membership, which Nicolas Sarkozy opposed (Accession to the EU, 18). A lack of consensus and strong resistance towards Turkey's membership by a number of member states, continues to hinder progression in the negotiation process.

Today, Turkey faces a Europe that is plagued with enlargement fatigue and immigration fatigue in the context of the economic downturn. Opposition expressed by European politicians, most notably those of Europe's biggest players Germany and France, reflects public opposition to Turkish accession in the context of a growing enlargement fatigue. The EU is hoped to be a group constructed around common values and norms facilitating compromise and consensus building and leading to the emergence of shared interests (Anvanitopoulos and Tzifakis, 2). This is expressed by the population in a 2006 Eurobarometer report which stated that in general citizens expect progress in European integration and collectivity on the world stage. Enlargement is worrisome in this context since it is perceived that enlargement represents a process of reconstructing the Union's own identity (Anvanitopoulos and Tzifakis, 12). It is being argued that, the larger and more diverse and less cohesive the EU becomes, so then its decision-making becomes more difficult and policy development more problematic (Tatham, 3). With Turkey's large population and its Muslim majority, Turkey represents the biggest threat to a cohesive, collective union. Moreover, enlargement fatigue is a result of the impression that enlargement causes the outsourcing of economic growth to new member states (Anvanitopoulos and Tzifakis, 14). Thus, opposition to Turkey arises from the worry that its membership would make Europe's current burdens heavier by straining an already limited budget, taxing an already troubled cultural identity further (Fsadni, 162). Thus, Turkey does not receive support from the European public as it is seen to represent a threat to cohesion of the already fragile Union both in terms of economic and cultural stability.

Moreover, the economic crisis has led to dissatisfaction toward immigration, thus opposition is often expressed, to Turkish accession in fear of large waves of Turkish immigrants.

In a Eurobarometer report in 2006 titled, *Eurobarometer 66: Public Opinion in the European Union,* when asked if immigrants contributed a lot to their countries, 52% disagreed with the statement and only 4 out of 10 EU citizens felt that immigrants made contributions. This is clearly indicative of a negative attitude among European citizens towards the immigrant population. The reason for this dissatisfaction was described in another Eurobarometer report titled *The European Citizens and the Future of Europe,* which cited that job precariousness in Europe was being attributed to competition from low labour cost countries. Thus, citizens are less likely to welcome immigrants in fear that they will take their jobs. Moreover, in a 2011 Eurobarometer report titled *Migrant Integration: Aggregate Report* expressed that many citizens had the impression that because of increased immigration, the social fabric is crumbling and national identity may become diluted and behavioural norms and values are being gradually lost. In this report, many of the interview participants expressed this concern specifically in regards to Turkish and Muslim immigrants. It found that many citizens have negative preconceptions of Turkish Muslim immigrants by holding an assumption that anyone who is Muslim is also a Terrorist. One participant stated that "Muslims in particular are portrayed as dangerous, stupid". This sentiment has been reflected in accession negotiations with Turkey since the free movement of workers in relation to the Muslim majority has been one of the most contentious conditions, as evidenced by the statement of Olli Rehn. Thus, public opposition is often expressed in opposition to a fear of Turkish immigration. It is feared that Turkey's Muslim population will overwhelm national and European identities.

The negotiations surrounding Turkey's accession is serving as 'litmus test' (Aydin, 181) for the enlargement of the EU. This is due to the fact that the current Europe is geared toward policy making based on easing social tensions and promoting social solidarity and cohesion (Keridis, 150), in the face of growing public discontent with the Union and tensions between national and immigrant populations. Turkey represents the perceived biggest threat to this need for social cohesion since in countries such as Germany and France, immigrant tensions are directed at the large Turkish and Muslim populations. If Turkey acceded to the Union, Europe would be more than a white Christian, in-ward looking club (Keridis, 155). For those who oppose Turkish accession, Turkey's perceived "Arab" and Muslim population threatens a European identity based on Judeo-Christian populations. Moreover, it is often argued that Islam is incompatible with the democratic values of Europe and that Islamic Culture is alien to Europe and the values that shape it (Keridis, 164). This presumption has been furthered by rising concerns that Muslims are unable to assimilate and accept European cultural norms (Tziampiris, 69). As declared by the likes of Giscard D'Estaing, Olli Rehn and Wilfried Martens, Turkey's Muslim population would thus mean the end of Europe. For those who view Turkey's accession favourably such as former British Foreign Secretary Jack Straw, integration would "prove how two cultures cannot only exist but thrive together in the modern world" (Keridis, 163). In this mindset, Turkey's accession would allow the European Union to project a larger influence in the world. Enlargement has often been used as a "powerful means of influencing much more than the immediate policies of third countries" (Arvanitopolous, 14). Thus, Turkey's accession would act as a bridge to the Middle East and may allow European influence to be diffused in the area. Evidently, the results of Turkish negotiations with the EU will determine whether Europe will choose an insular foreign policy, based on perceived shared common values, or if Europe will open its interaction and influence to a wider audience.

In conclusion, it seems that the hypothesis presented at the beginning of the paper, has largely been proven through the analysis of events. However, the hypothesis can be revised to include the material concerns relating to fears of the economic burden Turkey may present in the event of accession. Thus, this paper concludes that the European Union's decisions throughout negotiations of Turkey's integration with the community has been characterised by inconsistencies and contradictions, especially in comparison to other negotiating countries. These inconsistencies have been based on historical biases, perceptions that Turkey is not part of the European community, and fears of being overwhelmed culturally and economically, by Turkey. While there have been valid concerns raised about Turkey's ability to meet the economic, political and social criteria of membership, it is clear that these concerns are secondary to the overall opposition to Turkey's lack of "Europeaness." Moreover, these differences have been attributed to Turkey's perceived inability to adhere to European values of democracy and human rights. Countries that have acceded to the community throughout the duration of these negotiations, have benefitted from the consensus from member states, that their state belonged within their community, evidenced by statements in negotiation documents that declared their European identity. Turkey, on the other hand, has caused deep divisions within the community and has engendered strong oppositions to its candidacy, based on historical tensions, in the case of Greece and Cyprus, and identity politics in the case of France, Germany and Austria. Opposition from these countries have resulted in conditions being placed on Turkey's membership criteria, not placed on previous acceding states, and have consistently stalled the progress of negotiations. Negotiations have become increasingly difficult, as the possibility of Turkey's accession became more of a reality, rather than a distant proposition. As the negotiations moved from economic integration to a deeper integration into the structures of the community, opposition and identity politics became more pronounced and explicit. Moreover, Turkey's negotiations are being structured on Europe's willingness to receive the country, rather than Turkey's readiness for accession. Progress within the negotiations has not been a result of any progress in Turkey's ability to meet the criteria. Rather, real progress only came when European politics and public opinion softened towards the prospect of Turkish accession, such as in 1999. Thus, with Europe going through an economic and identity crisis which has led to enlargement and immigration fatigue hardening opposition to Turkish accession, negotiations are likely to only continue to be protracted and filled with extenuating conditions.

BIBLIOGRAPHY

"Agreement Establishing an Association between the European Economic Community and Turkey." *Official Journal of the European Communities* 16.No C 113 (1963)Print.

Arvanitopoulos, Constantine, Tzifakis, Nikolaos. "Introduction." *Turkey's Accession to the European Union: An Unusual Candidacy.* Ed. Nikolaos Tzifakis Constantine Arvanitopoulos. Athens: Centre for European Studies Publications, 2009. 1-8. Print. The Constantinos Karamanlis Institute for Democracy Series on European and International Affairs .

Avci, Gamze. "Putting the Turkish EU Candidacy into Context." *European Foreign Affairs Review* 7 (2002): 91-110. Print.

Aydin, Ali Ihasan. "Imagining the EU in the Turkish Mirror." *Turkey's Accession to the European Union: An Unusual Candidacy.* Ed. Nikolaos Tzifakis, Constantine Arvanitopoulos. Athens: Centre for European Studies Publications, 2009. 171-182. Print. The Constantinos Karamanlis Institute for Democracy Series on European and International Affairs.

Directorate General Communication. *Eurobarometer 66: Public Opinion in the European Union.* Autumn 2006 ed. 66 Vol. European Commission, 2006. Print.

---. The European Citizens and the Future of Europe: Qualitative Study in the 25 Member States.   Paris: European Commission, 2006. Print.

---. *Migrant Integration: Aggregate Report.* Qualitative Eurobarometer ed. European Commission, 2011. Print.

European Council in Copenhagen. *Conclusions of the Presidency – Copenhagen, June 21-22   1993* . Tran. European Council. Copenhagen:, 1993. Print.

Fsadni, Ranier. "The Debate's Impact on Europe." *Turkey's Accession to the European Union: An Unusual Candidacy.* Ed. Nikolaos Tzifakis, Constantine Arvanitopoulos. Athens: Centre for European Studies Publications, 2009. 159-170. Print. The Constantinos Karamanlis Institute for Democracy Series on European and International Affairs.

Keridis, Dimitris. "Turkey and the Identity of Europe: Contemporary Identity on the European   Frontier." *Turkey's Accession to the European Union: An Unusual Candidacy.* Ed.   Nikolaos Tzifakis, Constantine Arvanitopoulos. Athens: Centre for European Studies Publications, 2009.147-158. Print. The Constantinos Karamanlis Institute for Democracy Series on European and International Affairs.

Mayer, Matthias M. "Germany's Preferences on the Freedom of
Movement Provisions of the Ankara Agreement:
The Wirtschaftswunder and the Opportunity and Efforts of Turkish
Diplomacy". *European Union Studies Association, 11th Biennial
International Conference*. April 23rd - 25th, 2009, Marina Del
Rey, California. Archive of European Integration , 2009. Print.

Ruiz- Jiménez, and José I. Torreblanca. *European Public Opinion and
Turkey's Accession: Making Sense of Arguments*. Working
Paper ed. European Policy Institutes Network,   2007. Print.

Saatçioğlu, Beken. "Turkey- EU Relations from the 1960s- 2012: A
Critical   Overview." *Turkey's Accession to the European Union :
Political and Economic Challenges*. Eds. Belgin Akçay and Bahri
Yilmaz. Lanham, Maryland: Lexington   Books, 2013. 3-24.
Print.

Serdaroğlu, Ozan. "Fifty Years After the Ankara Agreement: The Need
for New   Commitments." *The Turkey Analyst* WEDNESDAY, 25
SEPTEMBER 2013 2013Print.

Sklias, Pantelis. "The Political Economy of Turkey's Accession to the
EU: A Comparative   Analysis." *Turkey's Accession to the
European Union: An Unusual Candidacy*. Ed.   Nikolaos Tzifakis,
Constantine Arvanitopoulos. Athens: Centre for European Studies
Publications, 2009.195-210. Print. The Constantinos Karamanlis
Institute for Democracy Series on European and International
Affairs.

Tatham, Allan F. *Enlargement of the European Union*. 4th ed. Austin:
Kluwer Law   International, 2009. Print. Kluwer European Law
Collection .

"Turkey and Europe: Just Not our Sort." *The Economist*, sec. Europe:Mar
13th 1997 1997. Print.   Westering, Jolanda Van. "Conditionality
and EU Membership: The Cases of Turkey and Cyprus." *European
Foreign Affairs Review* 5 (2000): 95-118. Print.

Tziampiris, Aristotle. "The European Union, Islam and Turkey: Delineating Europe's Soft   Power." *Turkey's Accession to the European Union: An Unusual Candidacy.* Ed.   Nikolaos Tzifakis, Constantine Arvanitopoulos. Athens: Centre for European Studies Publications, 2009.65-74. Print. The Constantinos Karamanlis Institute for Democracy Series on European and International Affairs

FOREIGN POLICY OBJECTIVES

4. FOREIGN POLICIES TO ACHIEVE DOMESTIC SECURITY

A POST-9/11 ANALYSIS
By: Sarah Frion

The concept of security, or more specifically domestic security, has evolved considerably over the past decades. I analyze how one aspect of the evolving understanding of security by posing the following question: *"how did the concept of domestic security become one that involves foreign policy?"* Domestic security can be understood through the definition used by the United States Department of Homeland Security who deem domestic security (or in their view Homeland Security) to be a national effort to prevent attacks from within a country. (Department of Homeland Security) On the other hand, foreign policies are normally those that adhere to the interest of a country at the international level. Linking the two together can seem to be incoherent due to one being at a domestic level and the other at the international level. To link the two concepts of security, I propose the following hypothesis: *Since September 11th, 2001, the governments of the United States of America and of France have decided to utilize foreign policy measures to achieve domestic security in light of the growing threat of transnational terrorism.* This hypothesis purports to establish a relation between the domestic and foreign interests after the tragic attack on U.S.A soil in 2001. I have chosen to do a two part analysis of the foreign policies and actions taken by the United States and France during a specific time period because the U.S. is a powerful country on the world stage and also an avid protestor against terrorism, and France is an important European Union and United Nations actor that has also voiced a lot of concern over the terrorism issue. I have chosen to use the terrorist attack of September 11th, 2001 as the starting point of my research since this event was the pivot point that turned a lot of attention towards terrorism as one of the greatest threat to domestic security. In order to narrow the time frame, I have chosen to analyze the foreign policy decisions of both countries with respect to the Afghanistan war in 2001 and the Iraq war in 2003.

I have organized my research, findings and analysis in the following manner: (1) in the first part, I analyze statements of leaders and/or government documents of both countries made right after the 9/11 attack to evaluate the language used in response to this attack; (2) in the second part, I enumerate and evaluate the foreign policies enacted by both countries to pursue domestic security, specifically in light of the wars in Afghanistan and Iraq; (3) and finally, in my conclusion, I evaluate my hypothesis.

Part 1 – Analysis of Language

This part consists of an analysis of the language used by the American and French Presidents in 2001 right after the 9/11 attack. In September, on the day of the attack, the President of the United States of America, George W. Bush, addressed his country, declaring that the U.S. would "make no distinctions between the terrorists who committed these acts and those who harbour them." (Bush, 2001) (Widmaier, 2007) This language could be interpreted as a narrow foreign policy directed to anyone who had any affiliation with the attack on U.S. soil. (Widmaier, 2007) His speech was directed solely at the perpetrators of 9/11 that posed a direct threat to the domestic security of the nation and should be stopped at any cost necessary. However, in Bush's second speech on September 20th,

2001 to Congress and the nation, the President portrays his country's interests more broadly targeting not only the perpetrators of the attack, but any terrorist group. This view can be seen when the President says in his speech: "Our war on terror begins with Al Qaeda, but it does not end there. It will not end until every terrorist group of global reach has been found, stopped and defeated."(Bush, 2001) Furthermore, it can be argued that when Bush says in the same speech, "The only way to defeat terrorism as a threat to our way of life is to stop it, eliminate it and destroy it where it grows. We will direct every resource at our command – every means of diplomacy, every tool of intelligence, every instrument of law enforcement, every financial influence, and every necessary weapon of war – to the destruction and to the defeat of the global terror network," (Bush, 2001) the president is changing the basic objectives of American foreign policy and making terrorism its' central focus. (Jones, n.d.) The change in the course of American foreign policy can be seen as going from pre-emptive action (relating to or constituting a military strike to gain advantage over an enemy that is perceived to be planning to attack) to preventive action (relating to preventing an enemy from conducting or carrying out any sort of attack); this is also known as the Bush Doctrine. (Jones, n.d.) The language used by Bush in both of the speeches right after 9/11 not only demonstrates a change in foreign policy, but also shows the President's willingness to utilize aggressive foreign policies to ensure his country's domestic security. In the following years, this aggressive view continued to grow in the United States; according to David Mitchell and Tansa Massoud,

> The implication of this new [aggressive] environment was reflected in the president's 2002 State of the Union address in which he

stated: "I will not wait on the events, while dangers gathers. I will not stand by, as peril draws closer and closer. The United States of America will not permit the world's most dangerous regimes to threaten us with the world's most destructive weapons. (Mitchel and Massoud, 2009)

President Bush continued to speak in a language that portrayed his intentions to use foreign policies or any means necessary to stop terrorists and ensure the security of the nation. According to the language, it can be argued that 9/11 became a huge pivot point in using threats to domestic security to legitimize the use of aggressive foreign policies towards perceived terrorists and according to Bush his strategy for fighting terrorists is "taking the fight to the terrorists themselves."(Bush, 2003)

In September 2001, the President of France was Jacques Chirac. Even though the September 11th attack was not on French soil, it still instilled fear in the population and especially the president. The fact that France has the largest Muslim population of any European country may also have played a role. In a press conference with Chirac and Bush in Paris on November 6th, 2001, Chirac said

... the fight against terrorism – and in this respect, we have similar understanding of what is being done and what should be done to fight and eradicate terrorism. [Bush and I] both know that terrorism still exists, that it can be active anywhere, at any time, and that, therefore, all leaders across the world must pay great attention to this issue and be determined to eradicate terrorism."(Bush and Chirac, 2002)

This statement shows Chirac as having the same opinion as Bush in terms of how to fight and when to fight terrorism for the sake of the security of their nations and their peoples. Both presidents agreed that after 9/11, combatting terrorism is their foreign policies' number one priority and that both countries will devote as much resources as possible to this fight.(Bush and Chirac, 2002) This conjoint speech demonstrates that both presidents were willing to enact foreign policy measures to eradicate the threat of terrorism to their respective countries' domestic security. President Chirac, in his speech at the 10th Ambassadors' Conference in August 2002, says that "[France] is still militarily active alongside the United States and her allies, since the war against Al-Qaeda isn't over and peace remains fragile and uncertain..." (United Nations, 2009) This statement shows that Chirac continues agree with Bush's view that foreign policies need to be directed at stopping terrorism at the source. However, in the same speech, Chirac leans towards multilateral diplomatic action in accordance with the United Nations and the Financial Action Task Force (FATF) to combat the financing of terrorism.(United Nations, 2009) This entails the beginning of a difference between the American interventionist view of the use of their foreign policies against the fight of terrorism and the French preference for diplomatic and multilateral means of implementation.

According to Paul Belkin, during this time period, French officials, including the President, realized that their military resources were not strong enough to fight on their own; therefore, their foreign policy needed to include a multilateral framework; that is to say, working with the European Union and the United Nations to ensure success in combatting terrorism.(Belkin, 2011) Therefore, the language used by the French President pertaining to his foreign policy objective can be seen as both coherent and as diverging from the Bush policy objectives in the sense that Chirac did want to intervene unilaterally in countries where terrorist groups were thought to reside. Unlike Bush who said he was willing to go at it alone, Chirac was reluctant to act without the accord of the United Nations.

Presidents Bush and Chirac both used language after 9/11 that pointed towards targeting their foreign policy objectives to the fight against terrorism to ensure both of their countries' domestic security. Paul Belkin writes that "Each [country] has recognized that terrorism [is] the most important threat to their security today."(Belkin, 2011) Therefore, the assumptions of my hypothesis seem to be correct in the sense that both governments decided to utilize foreign policy measures to fight transnational terrorism before it reaches their borders.

Part 2 – Foreign Policies Enacted

The two foreign wars on which I will be focusing my analysis are the war in Afghanistan in 2001 and the war in Iraq in 2003. Both France and the US participated in these wars to some extent, thus allowing for an analysis of their foreign policy objectives in each case.

(2)(a) The Afghanistan War -

After 9/11, the United States, under the Bush administration, attacked Afghanistan where the ruling Taliban were deemed to be aiding Al Qaeda.(Huddy and Feldman, 2011) The policy decision to go to war in Afghanistan against this group of terrorist pushed the Bush administration to, as the author Wesley Widmaier puts it, "advocate an increasingly crusading internationalism" which entails the intervention in another country to stop a perceived threat in that country.(Widmaier, 2007) A report of the National Commission on Terrorist Attacks upon the United States stated that Bush and his administration targeted the Taliban due to their perceived affiliation with Al Qaeda.(United States National Commission on Terrorist attacks, 2004) This persuaded Bush to order Secretary Rumsfeld to develop a military plan against the Taliban that included targets that would influence the Taliban's behavior.(United States National Commission on Terrorist attacks, 2004) The State Department was then tasked to deliver to the White House a report titled "Game Plan for a Political-Military Strategy for Pakistan and Afghanistan" which was directed at the Taliban to agree to certain U.S. demands that mostly related to Al Qaeda. This report was only designed to give a first attempt of diplomatic compliance; however, the Bush administration knew that the Taliban would not comply with these demands. Therefore, this gave the possibility for the U.S. State Department and Defense Department to obtain international support for a military intervention in Afghanistan. Without necessarily waiting for full support from international allies and the United Nations, the U.S. administration took a public stance "to use all its resources to eliminate terrorism as a threat [and] punish those responsible for the 9/11 attacks." (United States National Commission on Terrorist attacks, 2004) Bush and his administration then pushed for a military intervention in Afghanistan targeting the Taliban. A new directive called the National Security Presidential Directive 9 was passed titled

"Defeating the Terrorist Threat to the United States"; this directive extended to a global war on terrorism in which Al Qaeda was a main target but it targeted also any terrorist group that posed a threat to the United States; any country or organization that helped such terrorists should be aware that the United States will not distinguish between the two and will use military force to end all terrorist activities.(United States National Commission on Terrorist attacks, 2004) The directive was signed on October 26th, 2001 after American and allied troops had already been sent to Afghanistan to commence the war against the Taliban. This decision shows the use of foreign policy to ensure domestic security of the U.S. in regards to combatting terrorism.

Once the United States of America announced that they would be sending troops to Afghanistan to fight the global war on terror several other countries, including France, decided to do the same. On November 6th, 2001, President Jacques Chirac gave a speech answering some of the questions on the French involvement in Afghanistan. The most important aspect of this speech can be found in the following statement: "Finally, we discussed the internal security problems because you have to see one thing: we must understand that in reality, the purpose of a Head of State, when acting nationally or internationally, the ultimate responsibility is to ensure the security of its citizens, the security of its people."(United Nations, 2001) This is very important as it portrays one of Chirac's main reasons why he, along with his administration, had chosen to send troops in Afghanistan, to ensure the domestic security of his people. This view is in complete accordance with Bush's view of the necessity to go stop terrorist groups in Afghanistan to ensure domestic security in the U.S. The day after Chirac's speech, on November 7th 2001, the President announced publicly and officially the sending of French troops to Afghanistan to aid Americans in stopping the Taliban regime.(Le Nouvel Observateur, 2011)

Nevertheless, France's policy objectives in this war were not simply deemed to be based on security of the nation. The United Nations published on their website three reasons why the French were engaging in this war.(United Nations France, 2009) The first reason was France's respect for its international engagements with the United Nations as a permanent member of the Security Council, and its willingness to fight for human rights and women's rights as well. The second reason was to combat terrorism and to ensure that the Taliban do not take control over Afghanistan and become a sanctuary for terrorist organizations. The third reason was to ensure its own security by fighting against the constant threats of transnational terrorism.(United Nations France, 2009) Therefore, the foreign policy enacted in regards to the war in Afghanistan can be perceived to be an aid to ensure domestic security.   All in all, it is clear that the American and French governments both utilized their foreign policy objectives in this war to ensure the domestic security of their respective countries, a fact which supports my hypothesis.

(2)(b) Iraq War –

In the case of Iraq, the United States accused Iraq, more specifically its President Saddam Hussein, of being implicated in the 9/11 attack. However, due to the lack of evidence, Bush's administration put that claim aside and focused on Afghanistan until 2003.(Roberts, 2002) As there was no evidence of Iraq involvement in 9/11 or with the Taliban, the focus of the presumed Iraqi threat eventually resurfaced, this time with an emphasis on weapons of mass destruction. This claim became a new priority among Bush's foreign policy objectives. (United

States National Commission on Terrorist attacks, 2004) In October 2002, Bush argued on national television that Iraq had tried to purchase materials known to be used to construct weapons of mass destruction which pointed directly at Iraq becoming a bigger threat to the United States.(Widmaier, 2007) However, given the lack of proof that Saddam had even attempted to produce WMD's, Bush changed his position, stating that the United States foreign policy objective was to change the regime type in Iraq to safeguard the United States from a threatening regime, which he claimed to be the core purpose of invading Iraq.(Widmaier, 2007) Despite all kinds of international reluctance to go to war in Iraq, Bush and his administration deemed it to be the top priority of their foreign policies, and that determination led to the Iraq war.(United States Senate Intelligence Committee, 2008) In this example, it is difficult to analyze if this foreign policy enabled domestic security. However, it is unarguable that the Bush administration, regardless of their actual interests in this war, used the potential threat to domestic security from Iraq to pursue their foreign policy agenda.

While the United States insisted on going to war with Iraq, France, with other European allies, pressed the U.S. to confront this crisis within a multilateral framework.(Belkin, 2011) According Paul Belkin, "France was particularly critical [of the U.S. invasion of Iraq, which was seen as a unilateral action that undermined the notion of collective security."(Belkin, 2011) Chirac in a speech to the U.N. General Assembly pushed the notion that multilateralism is essential in times of crisis in order to preserve the security of all states. (De Villepin, 2003) This shows the French administration's reluctance to pursue foreign policies that are not designed in a multilateral framework. Chirac gave his direct opinion in the matter of the Iraq war in an interview with *Time* magazine, stating that "A war of this kind cannot help giving a big life to terrorism."(Graff and Crumley, 2003) In his opinion; this war could lead to even more terrorist outbreaks which could undermine the domestic security of any nation implicated in the war. He added that Iraq as of then posed no direct threat and he preferred to stick with the UN path of investigation before making wrong accusations which could result in Iraqi retaliation. (Graff and Crumley, 2003) These statements by the French President contradicted the American view and moved French foreign policy further toward acting in a multilateral framework, and away from Chirac's first point of view in the Afghanistan war in which the war would ensure France's domestic security. In this case, Chirac believed that war and an aggressive foreign policy, could lead to insecurities in the countries implicated. Therefore, Chirac's foreign policy decision to not go to war in Iraq further supports my hypothesis because France believed that if they enact the same foreign policy as the Americans, their domestic security could be undermined. Only this time, the implication for domestic security pointed French foreign policy in the opposite direction, away from direct military intervention and away from U.S. policy.

Conclusion

To recapitulate what my research has shown, the government of the United States of America, through the Afghanistan and Iraq wars, has utilized foreign policy measures in attempts to ensure its domestic security. Regardless of the criticisms of these two wars, the stance of the government was that aggressive or interventionist foreign policies ensure the security of the country from the threat of terrorist attacks. Therefore, in light of these two examples, my hypothesis seems to be valid. In the case of France, my hypothesis still applies, just in a different way. During the Afghanistan war, the French government's foreign policy was directed at intervening in Afghanistan to stop the threat of terrorism to ensure domestic security. Therefore, their choice of involvement with the U.S. proves my hypothesis to be correct. In the case of the Iraq war, France shifted its position on foreign policy measures. France officials did not perceive Iraq to be a threat, but instead believed aggressive foreign policy to be the source of threat to domestic security in the sense that it might create resentment which could lead the Iraqis and possibly others to retaliate. Therefore, the foreign policy decision of France to not act alongside the Americans in Iraq shows that in this instance as well, they had their domestic security in mind. My research thus clarifies further my hypothesis by showing a potential reason for a shift in France's attitudes between aggressive and restrained foreign policy measures in light of domestic security; if the threat is perceived to be imminent, then the foreign policy measures tend to be aggressive; if the threat is unclear, then the foreign policy measures tend to be restrained. However, which one is better; aggressive or restrained? In my opinion, both 'types' of foreign policies have in a sense ensured the security of both countries as there has not been another attack of such magnitude like 9/11. However, terrorist groups seem to continue to harbour hatred for the Western world and continue to attack on a smaller scale. Therefore, is it really possible to say that domestic security is ensured, or is it plausible to assume that another 9/11 type of attack may be imminent if some countries continue to pursue aggressive or restrained foreign policies?

BIBLIOGRAPHY

Journal Articles

Burcu, Savun, and Phillips Brian . "Democracy, Foreign Policy, and Terrorism." *Journal of Conflict Resolution.* 53.6 (December 2009): 878-904. Web. 24 Nov. 2013. <http://jcr.sagepub.com>.

Huddy, Leonie, and Stanley Feldman. "Americans Respond Politically to 9/11." *Understanding the Impact of the Terrorist Attacks and their Aftermath.* 66.6 (2011): 455-467.

Joseph Foxell, Jr. (2004) United States Policy on Terrorism: Where Are We Going and How Are We Getting There?, American Foreign Policy Interests: The Journal of the National Committee on American Foreign Policy, 26:3, 241-252

Mitchel, David, and Tansa Massoud. "Anatomy of Failure: Bush's Decision-Making Process in Iraq War."*Foreign Policy Analysis.* 5. (2009): 265-286. Web. 25 Nov. 2013.

Widmaier, Wesley. "Constructing Foreign Policy Crises: Interpretive Leadership in the Cold War and War on Terrorism." *International Studies Quaterly.* 51. (2007): 779-794.

Gouvernement Documents

Arens, Marianne, and Thull Francois. World Socialist Website. Comité Internationale de la Quatrième International. *La France participe à la guerre en Afghanistan et intensifie ses attaques contre les droits démocratiques.* 2001. Web. <http://www.wsws.org/francais/News/2001/novembre01/22nov01_1 oifrance.shtml>.

*Afghanistan : Conférence de presse de M. Jacques Chirac, Président de la République*France - ONU, 2001. Web. 25 Nov. 2013. <http://franceonu.org/la-france-a-l-onu/espace-presse/declarations-presse/points-de-presse/archives-1010/2006-2001/article/6-novembre-2001-afghanistan>

France - ONU. Le ministère des Affaires étrangères et européennes et le ministère de la Défense.*L'engagement de la France en Afghanistan*. 2009. Web. <http://www.franceonu.org/la-france-a-l-onu/un-express/article/l-engagement-de-la-france-en>.

George W. Bush: "The President's News Conference With President Jacques Chirac of France in Paris, France," May 26, 2002.Online by Gerhard Peters and John T. Woolley, *The American Presidency Project*. http://www.presidency.ucsb.edu/ws/?pid=63941. President Bush's address to a Joint Session of Congress, September 20, 2001 ; http://whitehouse.gov/news/releases/2001/09/20010920-8.html.

The White House President George W. Bush. *President Bush Releases National Strategy for Combating Terrorism*. Office of the Press Secretary, 2003. Web. <http://georgewbush-whitehouse.archives.gov/news/releases/2003/02/print/20030214-7.html>.

United Nations. *10th Ambassadors' Conference Speech by M. Jacques Chirac, President of the Republic*. 2009. <http://www.un.int/france/documents_anglais/020829_mae_chirac_general.htm>.

United States. National Commission on Terrorist Attacks Upon the United States. *Wartime*. 2004. Web. <http://www.9-11commission.gov/report/911Report_Ch10.htm>.

United States. Senate Intelligence Committee. *Two Bipartisan Reports Detail Administration Misstatements on Prewar Iraq Intelligence, and Inappropriate Intelligence Activities by Pentagon Policy Office*. Washington: 2008. http://www.intelligence.senate.gov/press/record.cfm?id=298775>.

News/Magazine Articles
Graff, James, and Bruce Crumley. "France is Not a Pacifist Country." *TIME Magazine*. 16 Feb 2003: n. page. Print. <http://content.time.com/time/magazine/article/0,9171,423466,00.html

Jones, Steve. "US Foreign Policy After 9/11: Obvious Changes, Subtle Similarities." *US Foreign Policy About.com.* n.d. n. page. Print. <http://usforeignpolicy.about.com/od/defense/a/Us-Foreign-Policy-After-9-11.htm>.

"Retour sur la présence française en Afghanistan depuis 2001." *Le Nouvel Observateur.* 14 07 2011: n. page. Web. 25 Nov. 2013. <http://tempsreel.nouvelobs.com/monde/20110713.OBS7010/retour -sur-la-presence-francaise-en-afghanistan-depuis-2001.html>.

Roberts, Joel. "Plans for Iraq attack began on 9/11." *CBC News.* 4 Sep 2002: n. page. Web. 25 Nov. 2013. <http://www.cbsnews.com/news/plans-for-iraq-attack-began-on-9-1

5. CYBER-SECURITY AND FOREIGN POLICY

ADDRESSING THE ROLE OF CYBER-SECURITY IN THE 21ST
CENTURY POLICY AGENDA
By: Easha Acharya

Introduction

Around the world, cyber-security is becoming an increasingly important item on the policy agendas of states. As nations are becoming more reliant on digital structures to perform legitimate business and government functions, governments are put in an unparalleled state of vulnerability. This reliance on information technology has left many vital interests susceptible to attacks. A distributed denial of service (DDoS) attack can shut down systems for extended periods of time which could potentially result in the loss of income, net worth, and jobs on an international scale (Himma 2007). What is even more alarming is the fact that a nation's vital infrastructure is at risk of shutting down at any given moment if digital information falls into the hands of rival and unfriendly organizations. It is an unsettling truth that a cyber-attack can potentially result in large-scale financial damage to a nation, and could even serve as a catalyst for "outright war" (Council on Foreign Relations 2013).

Where does this leave states in the struggle to balance the efficiency and economic advantages of becoming a 'digitalized state' with the best methods of national security and protection of their infrastructure? This paper will address this question in several ways. First, it will briefly look at the level of damage that a cyber-attack can have on a nation's functionality, using the 2007 Estonian cyber-attacks as a model. Then, it will look at how foreign pressures can affect the security measures needed to protect a nation's infrastructure. It will conclude with a look at which methods are most feasible for future adoption, taking into consideration potential foreign policy obstructions.

Part I: The New, Vulnerable State

In 1948, Hans Morgenthau predicted that national security would depend on the integrity of a nation's borders and its institutions (Geers 2011). However, as the vital infrastructures of states become more computerized and interconnected, the question of security exceeds by far a nation's physical boundaries. The US Department of Homeland Security has released some of the most detailed background information about this rapid digitalization of a state in reference to the United States. This document, the National Strategy to Secure Cyberspace went so far as to call the computerization of the United States an "Information Technology Revolution".

The term 'revolution' was used in reference to a mass shift in control of crucial manual and automated economic processes over to computerized networks. This shift occurred within the fields of manufacturing, utilities, as well as banking and communications. As a result, productivity and efficiency increased. By 2003, the United States' economy and its national security system had come to be almost entirely reliant on information technology and the "information infrastructure" (National Strategy, 2003: 1). On an even more intricate level, a network that consists of more complex networks singlehandedly sustains the operations of all sectors of the American economy: energy, electric power, all forms of transportation, finance, telecommunications, public health, emergency services, water, chemical, defense bases, food, agriculture, and postal services. They also control physical objects such as electrical transformers, trains, pipeline pumps, chemical vats, and radars (9).

As a result of this reliance on digital networks, the threat of cyber-attacks against the U.S. has evolved into one of the nation's most pressing national security issues, as discussed later in this analysis.

The centrality of state digitalization can also be seen in Iran, as a victim of the well-known Stuxnet virus. This virus was able to raise the pressure within nuclear reactors or shut down oil pipelines without notifying system operators. Once the virus was entrenched in a system, it did not necessarily activate. More precisely, it would only recognize a specific target. In this case, this target was the extractors that drive nuclear matter at Iran's enrichment facilities. Stuxnet was globally acknowledged to be the earliest weapon to consist entirely of computer code. The Washington-based Institute for Science and International Security stated that the virus had the potential to shut down 1,000 centrifuges at Natanz, which was Iran's chief enrichment facility in 2010, and that turning the plant on could have led to a national electricity blackout. Since the discovery of the virus, Iran put together the second-largest online security army in the world (Mitchell and Clair 1). The creation of this security army is a prime example of cyber-security shifting to the forefront of the national security itinerary.

The Estonian Case

The Estonian model is an exemplary case of how cyber-attacks can cripple a nation's infrastructure. It also leads into the discussion on how best to address the issue of national cyber-security. In April 2007, the Estonian government relocated the memorial statue of a soldier which commemorated the Soviet liberation of the country from the Nazi occupation. The aim of the relocation was to move the figure to an area which was less accessible and visible to the public (Herzog 2011). This act resulted in riots by Russophone groups and apparently also in an infamous act of cyber-terrorism which crippled Estonia's state-of-the art digital, economic, and political infrastructures (49).

The motivation behind the attack appeared to be retaliation for the removal of the statue. According to Herzog (2011), globalization and the Internet have enabled the Russian diaspora in Estonia to "threaten the sovereignty of nation-states in cyberspace" (54). He points out that those behind the attack were in possession of skills and technology which make them essentially untraceable. The extent of their abilities could disrupt or devastate government operations, banking processes, urban power grids, and military weapon systems (1). According to Herzog, the cyber-attacks on Estonia transpired in the midst of tense conditions between resident Estonians and the nation's Russian minority population. He describes the situation:

On April 30, 2007, the government moved the Bronze Soldier, a decision [which] sparked rioting among the Russian-speaking community...In addition to rioting and violence from April 27 to May 18, distributed denial-of-service (DDoS) cyber-attacks target[ed] the country's infrastructure...Estonian officials like Foreign Minister Urmas Paet quickly accused Russia of perpetrating the attacks, but European Commission and NATO technical experts were unable to find credible evidence of Kremlin participation in the DDoS strikes (51).

The implications for Estonia's economy and its foreign relations were extensive, and the effects were seen immediately. Service became unavailable for members of the public, in regards to banking and intradepartmental government communications. In a country where ninety-five percent of banking transactions are done through electronic means, one can imagine the cost that the loss of services brought about (Ashmore 2009). Major setbacks included the shutdown of the websites of all government bureaus, the two largest banks, and several political parties. As well, the parliamentary email server was disabled (Herzog 2011).

As for foreign relations, there was no consensus around the origin of the attacks, and the speculations that the attack came from Russia caused even more tension in an already uneasy relationship between Estonia and Russia, with accusations stemming directly from the Estonian Prime Minister, Andrus Ansip (Ashmore 2009). Although a Russian IP address was identified in the investigation, there was insufficient evidence to ascertain a definitive Russian contribution to the attack. This problem of identifying the source of an attack further emphasizes the sophistication of cyber-attacks. The perpetrators, whether they are individuals or states, can be protected by the difficulty of tracking and the intricacy of systems.

In the short term, the Estonian government's reactions included the establishment of the Estonian Information Systems Authority (RIA). As well, the Estonian Ministry of Economic Affairs and Communications enhanced the role of the National Cyber Security Council which aims to foster communications between security analysts, computer experts, lawyers, diplomats, and regulators. The National Cyber Security Council also supports the creation of a nation-wide early warning system in conjunction with well-regarded digital security companies (Raud n.d.). Another result of the attacks was the decision of Estonia's President, Foreign Minister, and Defense Minister to raise the emergency with their EU and NATO colleagues. However the response was bleak: the Estonian Defense Minister of the time, Jaak Aaviksoo stated "at present, NATO does not define cyber-attacks as a clear military action. This means that the provision of Article V of the North Atlantic Treaty, or in other words collective self-defense, will not automatically be extended to the attacked country"(Traynor 2007). His statement is legitimized by the fact that although collective defense continues to be viewed as a mature approach to cyber-security, this possibility is made difficult by the too-common lack of a conclusive aggressor in cyber-attacks.

Part II: Proposed Resolutions

The Estonian incident has furthered the debate on cyber-security defense solutions. The most highly proposed approaches to cyber defense have integrated at least some element of international cooperation, or cyber-defense through alliances. According to Alex Kinsgsbury (2008) "the international community urgently needs to establish legal norms when it comes to computer and online crimes to help define and deter a problem that is escalating in severity" and that the best way to do this would be to look toward groups such as NATO and the European Union. Ashmore (2009) discusses the merits of alliances such as NATO in respect to cyber-security and whether the framework of NATO is appropriate for cyber defence. Stating that "cyber defence is a critical issue for NATO", Ashmore articulates that despite a significant push for NATO as a resolution for cyber-security, it would be difficult to treat cyber-attacks in the same way as an act of war. He quotes a senior NATO official: "If a member state's communications centre is attacked with a missile, you call it an act of war. So what do you call it if the same installation is disabled with a cyber-attack?"

Ashmore raises an important question; however, his description of NATO's cyber strategy almost certainly confirms NATO's current framework as unsuitable for dealing with a cyber-attack on a member state. NATO's current cyber strategy is focused on protecting its own, central infrastructure and intelligence, not the extensive information and infrastructure contained within each of its member states. In order for NATO to be a part of a solution to cyber-attacks on member states' infrastructure, the alliance would have to spend years developing a new strategy which encompasses and connects the cyber security system of each member state – a complicated and time-consuming endeavour. Furthermore, at present, not all NATO countries have legal definitions for cyber-crimes. In order for allied cooperation to be a realistic possibility, states need to first create laws that definitively encompass specific cyber-crimes and their respective sentences. Legal grey areas only leave room for greater incentive for cyber-attacks and diminish security possibilities.

Other collaborations have been proposed as well, such as the notion of collective cyber-security through the members of the UKUSA agreement. Former U.S. Homeland Security Secretary Janet Napolitano proposed this idea at the U.S. Naval Postgraduate School in California in in July 2012. However, not everyone agrees that this would be a suitable solution. According to Ian Wallace of the Brookings Institution, "The great Catch-22 of cyber-related diplomacy is that while everyone acknowledges the importance of international cooperation, there is rarely sufficient trust between countries to enable a meaningful discussion" (Wallace 2013). Wallace's comments once again stress the idea that cyber-security is an issue of which the intangibility eludes the once-strategic effects of 20th-century military solutions. So, factoring out imminent collective defense, where does this leave a global leader such as the United States in terms of effectively addressing cyber-security issues? Before I tackle this question, I must consider another point: America's biggest obstacle to self-sustained cyber-security are foreign pressures.

Part III: Foreign Policy Connections: The Example of the US

The United States' government has not underestimated the scope of cyber-security as has been evident since the release of its 2013 document 'Presidential Policy Directive 20' which consists of 'Offensive Cyber Effects Operations' that "offer unique and unconventional capabilities to advance U.S. national objectives around the world with "little or no warning to the adversary or target and with potential effects ranging from subtle to severely damaging"(Greenwald and MacAskill 2013). The document also says the government will "identify potential targets of national importance where OCEO can offer a favourable balance of effectiveness and risk as compared with other instruments of national power". However, American cyber-security efforts have been limited.

Fatefully, one of the world's most technologically advanced countries is fighting to safeguard both itself and its interests in the realm of digital disputes. Recent affairs prove that cyber threats are increasing in both quantity and sophistication, but simultaneously, the potential for security milestones in American cyber-defense has been highly constrained by political pressures from overseas. As Dallin McKinnon wrote for the American security journal *Praemon,* "domestic and foreign political pressures have largely tied officials' hands" (McKinnon 2013).

The National Security Agency, which is frequently viewed as a gold standard organization in pioneering cyber-security, is currently confronting endless obstacles as it aims to uphold, as well as enlarge its operations. Its scheme to launch a vast nationwide digital defense system was disrupted by the Snowden leaks. This led to angry backlash from multiple states, including Mexico, Brazil, and many European Union countries, which have similarly pressured the agency to cut back its surveillance plans. Furthermore, this has discouraged Congress from dealing with imperative cyber-security legislation in 2013. As social viewpoints on personal privacy become more of a concern, a consensus on balancing privacy and security issues has been difficult to find. Furthermore, the 2013 government shutdown over the federal budget led to a decrease of federal cyber-security programs. Such disruptions prevent the emergence of innovative contribution to government cyber plans and strategies. As a result, the countless political pressures at both the domestic and international levels have prevented speedy developments of the United States' cyber defense initiatives. (McKinnon 2013)

These obstructions to the expansion of American cyber-security initiatives have put the nation in an uneasy place. Because the intensity of cyber threats continues to evolve at a rapid pace, any halt of its in cyber capabilities leaves the United States at a disadvantage, a deep burden on state security. As McKinnon (2013) mentions, "the stakes are higher now because not only do adversaries like China, Russia, and Iran have sophisticated cyber capabilities, but these same technologies are also on track to become available to non-state actors like terrorist groups". But the country will also continue to have to handle cyber threats from state actors. The lack of functional cyber-security legislation, paired with the restrictive results that stem from the unending political pressure from foreign nations could give competitor states extra reason and opportunity to target American infrastructure.

The question of whether the United States' current reservation of the right to retaliate with military force against a cyber-attack is their best option is difficult to answer. I believe that it would be difficult to attach a military response to cyber-crimes because even if an attacker is identified, it would be a complicated task to determine a military action accordingly, and with proportionality. Although the United States was not conclusively determined to have played a role in the development of the Stuxnet worm against Iran, one can only speculate the reaction if Iran authorized a military response in retaliation to such an intangible act. What is more viable, as Rachel King wrote for CBS, is an idea which many cyber-security experts are predicting, of a "digital arms race" in which states scramble for a technological advantage (King 2012). The lack of current legal boundaries still gives the advantage to non-state actors, which in itself is neither good nor bad, but makes response on the state level more problematic.

Right now, the United States also needs to devote more resources and attention to cyber defense programs. The etiquette in the execution of these plans is complicated; still, the nation must find a way to stimulate modernization of its cyber capabilities. Since the effectiveness of cyber defense rests on constant digital upkeep, it is critical that the U.S. shield this division of Homeland Security from, as McKinnon puts it "across-the-board financial cuts like sequestration" (McKinnon 2013). He goes on to state "a voluntary information-sharing framework already exists, but Congress should strengthen this model through more forceful legislation" . This insight is correct, but it is also incredibly time-sensitive. While a huge cyber-attack like the one in Estonia has not occurred again, the possibility of it and the potential cost does get higher with each passing year. As such, the growing sophistication of cyber-attacks makes the creation of new legislation an urgent task.

Part IV: Conclusions

The fact that even the technologically most advanced economy, that of the United States, has difficulty both in protecting its cyber-security as well as agreeing on the measures that might be needed to enhance such security is ample demonstration of how difficult a subject this is for contemporary states. If the U.S. cannot achieve cyber-security, what chance do Estonia or Iran have to do so? Traditional international organizations such as the UN and NATO have also barely touched on the subject of cyber-security, a subject which falls outside the framework of the international system within which they were created. Information technology specialists, international law experts and the United Nations and its members have a lot of work ahead of them before they can define and then provide regulations which include cyber-security in the existing system of international governance.

BIBLIOGRAPHY

Himma, Kenneth Einar. Internet Security: Hacking, Counterhacking, and Society. 1. Seattle: Jones & Bartlett Learning, 2007. Print.

Geers, Kenneth. "Strategic Cyber Security." NATO Cooperative Cyber Defense Centre of Excellence. (2011): n. page. Print.

"Council on Foreign Relations." Cyberconflict and Cybersecurity Initiative. Council on Foreign Relations. Web. 26 Nov 2013. <http://www.cfr.org/projects/world/cyberconflict-and-cybersecurity-initiative/pr1497>.

Schmidt, Howard A. , and Richard A. Clarke . United States. US-CERT. National Strategy to Secure Cyberspace . Washington DC: , 2003. Print.

Clair, Patrick, and Scott Mitchell. "Stuxnet: Anatomy of a Computer Virus." Stuxnet: Anatomy of a Computer Virus. ABC1 Sydney :

Herzog, Stephen. "Revisiting the Estonian Cyber Attacks:." Journal of Strategic Security. 4.2 (2011): n. page. Print.

Ashmore , William. "Impact of Alleged Russian Cyber Attacks." School of Advanced Military Studies. (2009): n. page. Print.

Raud , Helena. Estonia. Ministry of Economic Affairs and Communications. Cyber Security in Estonia: A National Response in the New Risk Environment. Print.

Traynor, Ian. "Russia accused of unleashing cyberwar to disable Estonia." Guardian. 17 5 2007: n. page. Web. 26 Nov. 2013.

Kingsbury, Alex. "When Do Online Attacks Cross the Line Into Cyberwar?." US News. 9 12 2008: n. page. Web. 26 Nov. 2013.

Wallace, Ian. "Cyberwar: Leveraging old ties for new threats." Interpreter. (2013): n. page. Web. 26 Nov. 2013.

Greenwald, Glenn, and Ewen MacAskill . "Obama orders US to draw up overseas target list for cyber attacks." Guardian. 7 6 2013: n. page. Web. 26 Nov. 2013.

King, Rachel. "Most Cyber Security Experts Believe Cyber Arms Race is On." CBS News [New York] 30 01 2012, n. pag. Web. 26 Nov. 2013.

McKinnon, Dallin. "The State of American Cyber Security." Praemon. (2013): 1-4. Web. 26 Nov. 2013.

FOREIGN POLICY OF
MIDDLE POWERS

6. CANADIAN FOREIGN POLICY AND THE CRISIS IN DARFUR
By: Emily Preston

In February 2003, the Sudan Liberation Army and the Justice and Equality party attacked government offices and facilities in west Sudan. In response, the government of Sudan organized a militia called the Janjaweed that began a campaign of rape, murder, torture, and forced displacement in the Darfur region of west Sudan. These human rights abuses received little international attention until March 2004 when the United Nations Human Rights Coordinator for Sudan gave a speech detailing the situation in Darfur. The purpose of this paper is to analyze the Canadian foreign policy response to the crisis in Darfur between 2003 and 2006. The hypothesis of my research is that Canadian policy and decision-making regarding the crisis in Darfur was not formulated quickly enough, and that the Canadian implementation of that policy was not as effective as might have been expected, given the strength of the language in official policy and government statements.

The initial Canadian response to the crisis in Sudan was based on the concepts of the responsibility to protect and humanitarian intervention. The responsibility to protect is based on the idea that states are responsible for the welfare of their and other citizens, and the international community can violate state sovereignty in order to address human rights abuses or crises within a state when its own government fails to act. According to Paul D. Williams and Alex J. Bellamy, the crisis in Darfur qualifies for humanitarian intervention because it meets the "threshold criteria- 'large scale loss of life' and 'large scale ethnic cleansing' - that must be met before the 'responsibility to protect' can be invoked to override state sovereignty." (Williams and Bellamy 2005) However, instead of calling for a full humanitarian intervention, the United Nations passed several resolutions, such as Resolution 1556, Resolution 1590, Resolution 1591, and Resolution 1593. Resolution 1556 "made a series of demands on the Sudanese government, the most important of which were to disarm the militias and to bring to justice those responsible for the atrocities committed against the people in Darfur." (Riddell-Dixon 2004) Resolution 1556 also threatened the government of Sudan with sanctions if it did not comply. Sanctions were then put in place by Resolution 1591, which also created an arms embargo on the forces fighting in Darfur, including non-governmental actors and included the government of Sudan. (Riddell-Dixon, 2004) Resolution 1590 did not address Darfur as such; it focused on peace throughout Sudan. (Riddell-Dixon 2004) Resolution 1593 "[referred] the situation in Darfur to the International Criminal Court." (Riddell-Dixon 2004).

The African Union Mission in Sudan (AMIS) deployed 432 troops in 2004 with the intention of increasing that number by several thousand troops by September 2005. (Black 2010) The deployment of such a small number of troops is not in line with the rhetoric coming from Prime Minister Martin at the time, and is clearly 'minimalist'. (Black 2010) The concept of the responsibility to protect was not internationally implemented at the time that the crisis in Darfur began, though it did have an important influence on how the Canadian government approached the crisis. The response from the United Nations is also a factor, because the Canadian government's agency was limited in how it could approach the crisis.

The individual responsible for Canadian policy regarding the crisis in Darfur was former Prime Minister Paul Martin, who held the office from 2003-2006. Kim Richard Nossal states that one of

Paul Martin's main policy concerns as Prime Minister was humanitarian intervention. (Nossal 2005) In March of 2004, Martin gave a speech to the Davos World Economic Forum arguing that Canada's position was that the international community needs to change rules regarding sovereignty in order to intervene in humanitarian crises. (Nossa, 2005) However, Nossal also argued that "The Prime Minister's rhetoric about Canada's concern for the humanitarian crisis became so inflated that it was impossible for the government to ensure that its actions matched its rhetoric." (Nossal 2005) This had a large impact on the Canadian response to the crisis in Darfur, as the level of rhetoric made the Canadian response look limited and disappointing.

For example, the 2005 Canadian International Policy statement discusses Canada's policy toward Darfur:

> Canada is adopting a "whole of Sudan" strategy, whereby activities targeted to specific regions, such as Darfur, are developed and implemented within the context of their impact throughout Sudan. Canada's activities in Darfur are based on the 3D approach involving diplomatic activity, development and humanitarian aid, and support for improving the security situation through defence and civilian police involvement. Since 2000, Canada has contributed $70 million in humanitarian aid and $20 million in support to the African Union mission in Sudan, which is deployed in Darfur. Our contribution to the African Union includes helicopter support, which is considered the backbone of the operation, critical military and civilian police staff support to assist in planning, and military equipment for the African Union troops. Canada is examining the scope for a bigger role in the

Darfur crisis." (Canada's International Policy Statement 2005:10-11)

This document outlines Canada's specific strategy regarding the crisis in Darfur, and its emphasis on diplomacy and humanitarian aid. It emphasizes the approach Martin advocated: a focus on humanitarian intervention and aid. The implementation of this strategy and criticisms of the Canadian approach are discussed below.

Domestic politics had an influence on Canadian policy regarding Darfur, as is noted by both David Black (2005) and Kim Nossal (2005), The Martin government was facing a non-confidence motion, and as a minority government, needed public and parliamentary support. In order to help pass the budget in 2005, and gain favour among Members of Parliament and the public, Martin announced an assortment of new measures geared towards the crisis in Darfur:

> On 12 May, one week before the expected budget vote, Martin announced the enhanced Darfur package that included $170 million in support of the African Union mission in Sudan, and $28 million in aid for Darfur channelled through international agencies operating in Darfur and Chad. In addition, Martin authorized up to 100 additional officers to be deployed to Sudan to assist the African Union force. He also appointed a special "advisory team" to coordinate Canadian efforts on the Darfur file consisting of Robert Fowler, his personal representative for Africa, Senator Mobina Jaffer, Canada's special envoy for peace in Sudan, and Romeo Dallaire, whom Martin had appointed to the senate as a Liberal on 24 March." (2005)

However, this offer was then rejected by the ambassador from Sudan, because the African Union and Sudan did not want non-African soldiers in Darfur (Nossal 2005). Once the crisis in Parliament had passed, this package regarding Darfur was not re-evaluated and amended, other than a statement that said Canadian troops in Sudan would be unarmed. (Nossal 2005)

This aid package and how it was presented and subsequently amended shows that there was a disconnect between what the Canadian government was saying, and what it was actually doing in order to address the humanitarian crisis in Darfur. The Canadian government chose to respect the sovereignty of the government of Sudan, despite serious human rights abuses, and chose not to push for international humanitarian intervention. When it comes to the timing of Canada's contribution, it was 2006 before any real change in humanitarian aid to Sudan occurred, as can be seen in the graph below.

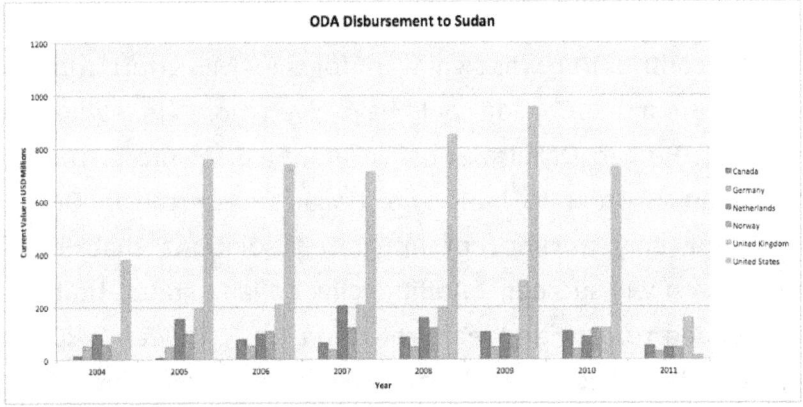

Fig. 1: ODA Disbursement to Sudan from Canada, Germany, the Netherlands, Norway, the United States and the United Kingdom: 2004-2011. Source OECD (2013) (See Appendix for exact figures)

According to the OECD data shown above, Canada contributed approximately $13 million dollars (USD) to Sudan in humanitarian aid in 2004, and $7 million dollars (USD) in 2005.

This number does not increase substantially until 2006, when Canada gave approximately $75 million dollars (USD) of humanitarian aid to Sudan. This amount is composed of direct monetary aid given to Sudan from Canada. This does not account for Canada's contributions to AMIS, which consisted of equipment:

> Canadian support to AMIS began in 2004 with a contribution of basic army equipment, including helmets, body armour and maps. In 2005, this initial endowment was followed by the loan of 105 armoured vehicles to three African nations contributing troops to AMIS: Senegal, Rwanda and Nigeria. From December 31, 2007, to June 30, 2009, Canada extended this loan for the three countries to continue to use armoured vehicles as part of UNAMID (Foreign Affairs Canada)

This contribution was significant for the AMIS effort, though it can be argued that Canada could have given more aid, equipment, or troops. Romeo Dallaire specifically argued for more troops in the region in order to intervene. Dallaire "asserted in October 2004 that only a series of integrated solutions that include intervention will succeed". Additionally, Dallaire stated that what was needed to provide "real protection was between 24,000 to 44,000 well-trained and well-equipped troops, preferably a mix of AU and NATO troops or AU and Western troops." (Totten 2009) Dallaire was one of the members of the special advisory team created by Martin in 2005, but as is discussed below, this approach towards the crisis was not implemented, and aid did not increase substantially until 2006.

The Canadian government also made a pledge of $90 million dollars as aid to Sudan following a World Bank/UN assessment in

Oslo in 2005, and stated that "[t]hese funds are to be distributed among three broad categories of programs: efforts to sustain peace and reduce poverty ($40 million); the immediate needs of the Sudanese people ($40 million); and contributions to peacebuilding and governance ($lo million)." (Matthews 2004) This pledge, however, becomes less impressive when one looks the pledges made by other states:

> The United States led the pack offering $850 million right away, with an additional $900 million depending on the support of Congress, which is likely to be influenced in its deliberations by whether or not the violence and atrocities in Darfur have ended. The U.S. was followed by the European Union, the United Kingdom, Norway, and the Netherlands with pledges of $765 million, $545 million, $250 million, and $220 million respectively. It is, of course, one thing to make a pledge and another to honour that pledge with actual cash. (Matthews 2004)

As can be seen, Canada's contribution was minimal in comparison to that of other smaller states such as Norway and the Netherlands. Matthews is right in pointing out that these are merely pledges, and some states may not have actually given as much as they pledged. However, the OECD data shown above clearly shows that Canada consistently gave less than Norway, the Netherlands, and the United Kingdom.

Criticisms of the Canadian response to the crisis in Darfur

David Black (2007) argues that Canada "has fallen short of the expectation of leadership role to which its own previous statements and actions have given rise." This reflects the argument also put forward by Nossal regarding "ear candy" (2005). Also similarly to Nossal, Black argues that Canadian domestic politics played a role in Canada's decision to offer a larger amount of aid to Darfur, as the Martin government was then facing a budget vote that could lead to a non-confidence motion. Black also states that Canada played a diplomatic role in the signing of the Darfur Peace Agreement in 2006. (Black 2007) Black criticises the Harper government's decision to disband the Special Advisory Team put in place by Paul Martin that consisted of Romeo Dallaire, Senator Mobina Jaffer (who was also Canada's Special Envoy for Peace in Sudan) and Ambassador Robert Fowler, and the resistance to "pre-commit substantial forces ('boots on the ground') to the enlarged UN-AU force mandated by last August's Resolution 1706". (Black 2007) In 2006, when Stephen Harper replaced Paul Martin as Prime minister, he emphasized the war in Afghanistan over the crisis in Darfur.

According to Elizabeth Riddell-Dixon (2004), Canada gave a substantial amount of money to the African Union in order to support peacekeeping efforts in Darfur. However, Riddell-Dixon states that Canada could have given more. Considering the level of rhetoric noted by Black and Nossal, Canada would most likely have contributed to a peacekeeping mission based on the tenets of R2P if the United Nations had passed a requisite resolution. That resolution was never passed, and all of the rhetoric used by the Prime Minister became empty words that were not supported by a large contribution to end the crisis. If the Prime Minister had followed his own rhetoric, it is more likely that he would have pushed for more humanitarian intervention despite the infringement on state sovereignty.

Martin's rhetoric frequently called for the Canadian response to be clear, decisive, and extensive. What was put in place in 2004 did not reflect this. Following this announcement, Canadian policy was criticized by Romeo Dallaire and David Kilgour (an MP from

Alberta). (Nossal 2005) These criticisms led to an increase of Canadian contributions to Darfur:

> Stung by this criticism, the government immediately increased Canada's commitment; on 10 September 2005, the minister of foreign affairs, Pierre Pettigrew, and the minister of international cooperation, Aileen Carroll, announced a spending package of $1 million designed to support a variety of human rights protection initiatives in Darfur, including funding to the UN office of the high commissioner for human rights to enable it to expand its operations in western Sudan and funding for the African Union's special representative for protection of civilians in armed conflict. (Nossal, 2005).

Evidently, public perception and criticism also played a role in how the Canadian government addressed the crisis in Darfur. The criticisms made by Kilgour and Dallaire were influential, because following their statements the Canadian government made more of an effort to address the crisis. Prime Minister Martin also used the aid package announced in 2005 in an attempt to gain favour with Kilgour, in order to get him to support the Martin government's budget (Nossal 2005) This reinforces the idea that the Canadian response was not solely based on humanitarian intervention but also by domestic politics.

According to Matthews, "Canada's policy towards the peacebuilding process in Sudan... lacks in generosity." (Matthews, 2005) Matthews also states that Canada's policy towards Sudan is focused on short-term goals, "such as mine clearance, refugee repatriation, and good governance." (Matthews 2005) He is also critical of the decision to "reduce the number of countries that would receive Canadian assistance in the future to 25" (Matthews

2005) because Sudan is unlikely to receive funding for long-term needs. This criticism can be countered, as can the criticisms made by Black regarding Prime Minister Harper, because Canadian aid to Sudan did not decrease following the election of Prime Minister Harper in 2006. In fact, aid to Sudan increased in the years 2008-2010 (see graph above). However, as is noted by Black and Williams, Canada did not commit troops to a later "UN-AU force mandated by Security Council resolution 1706 of August 2006 ('boots on the ground')." (Black and William0073 241) This took place after Prime Minister Stephen Harper took office, and shows the shift in goals and policy focus from that of Paul Martin's government.

Nossal's main criticism is that "[t]he manifest unwillingness of the Canadian government to go beyond token symbolism in addressing the massive killings in Darfur while engaging in inflated and self-congratulatory rhetoric demonstrates clearly that in contemporary Canadian foreign policy, what matters is not what one does, but only what one says." (Nossal 2005) The Canadian rhetoric as announced by Romeo Dallaire and Paul Martin regarding humanitarian intervention and the responsibility to protect, called for a large scale intervention and large amounts of aid. However, the Canadian response was limited and, as noted by Riddell-Dixon and Matthews, lacking in generosity in comparison to that of other smaller states.

The counter argument that defends Canada's contribution to the crisis in Darfur states that Canada was restricted by the African Union, the government of Sudan, and the inability of the UN Security Council to pass a resolution that would require humanitarian intervention of the scale that individuals like Romeo Dallaire were advocating. Tom Keating quotes Tim Shaw and David Black in saying that "Canada has not been an insignificant player in the uneven global response to the crisis. Yet the net effect has been to help sustain a starkly inadequate effort, especially when measured against the emerging standard of R2P." (Keating 2012) Additionally, as has already been noted, the Canadian government chose to respect the sovereignty of Sudan when it rejected the Canadian aid package offered in 2005, on the grounds that Sudan did not want armed non-African troops in the region.

Conclusion

Evidently, my hypothesis has been proven. The Canadian response lacked generosity in comparison to that of other states, and was based at times on self-interest as opposed to the concepts of humanitarian intervention and the responsibility to protect. The Canadian government did not live up to its rhetoric that invoked these concepts, as it respected the sovereignty of the government of Sudan instead of pushing for an intervention. Canada did face obstacles which limited the scope of its response, such as the restrictions on non-African troops put in place by the African Union, the inability of the United Nations to pass a resolution to call for humanitarian intervention, and the reluctance of the international community to violate state sovereignty in order to address serious human rights abuses. Yet the Canadian government could have done more, and given more, in order to address this crisis. The Canadian contribution to AMIS, diplomatic efforts to help the Darfur Peace Agreement in 2006, and the humanitarian aid given, were all good efforts, but not enough in the face of such a serious humanitarian crisis.

Appendix

QWIDS Query Wizard for International Development Statistics							
Time Period Donor(s)	2004	2005	2006	2007	2008	2009	2010	2011
Canada	13.389363	7.276552	75.228259	63.605677	83.448155	105.145136	108.273022	52.33773
Germany	48.247223	44.895423	50.71971	36.930793	47.300283	47.221828	39.183846	29.60158
Netherlands	97.7221	154.771	96.07874	202.51158	157.586	97.32924	86.710725	45.383343
Norway	57.30699	98.741265	108.005395	119.711601	119.84049	92.089886	116.69629	46.960891
United Kingdom	90.032821	196.071622	209.275167	206.17103	199.237092	295.923541	119.291796	158.940522
United States	377.534	758.97	738.663	710.459656	848.151677	954.628257	726.348228	16.448822

OECD Query Wizard Data for this table can be accessed at:
<<http://stats.oecd.org>> (Accessed November 24th, 2013)

BIBLIOGRAPHY

Books

Black, David R. "Canada" in *The International Politics of Mass Atrocities: The Case of Darfur*. Eds. David R. Black and Paul Williams. London ; New York: Routledge, 2010.

Keating, Tom "Mobilising the Troops"Knight, *The Routledge Handbook of the Responsibility to Protect*. Eds. W. Andy., and Frazer Egerton. New York: Routledge, 2012.

Totten, Samuel "Saving Lives in Darfur, 2003-06?: Lots of Talk, Little to No Action" in *The World and Darfur : International Response to Crimes Against Humanity in Western Sudan*. Ed. Amanda Grzyb. Montreal, QC, CAN: McGill-Queen's University Press, 2009.

Journal Articles

Black, David. "The Responsibility To Engage: Canada And The Ongoing Crisis In Darfur." *Behind the Headlines* 64.4 (2007): 17-23.

Matthews, Robert O. "Sudan's Humanitarian Disaster-Will Canada Live up to Its Responsibility to Protect." *Int'l J.* 60 (2004): 1049-1064

Nossal, Kim Richard "Ear Candy: Canadian Policy toward Humanitarian Intervention and Atrocity Crimes in Darfur". *International Journal* , Vol. 60.4 (Autumn, 2005), pp. 1017-1032

Riddell-Dixon, Elizabeth. "Canada's Human Security Agenda-Walking the Talk." *Intternational Journal* 60   (2004): 1067-1092

Williams, Paul D., and Alex J. Bellamy. "The responsibility to protect and the crisis in Darfur." *Security Dialogue* 36.1 (2005): 27-47.

Websites
"Canada's international policy statement: A role of pride and influence in the world," overview booklet, Ottawa, 2005.
<<www.international.gc.ca>>

Organisation for Economic Co-operation and Development *ODA Disbursement to Sudan from Canada, Germany, the Netherlands, Norway, the United States and the United Kingdom: 2004-2011.* Collected using the "Query Wizard for International Development Statistics"
<<http://stats.oecd.org>>_ Accessed November 24th, 2013

7. HUMAN SECURITY IN SUB-SAHARAN AFRICA
By: Marie-Pascale Poku

"Human Security is intended to meet the needs of the most vulnerable individuals and groups by protecting Human Rights and promoting political inclusion, the environment, health, development and to alleviate poverty" (Abubakar,7-8).

If the security of Sub-Saharan Africans is not threatened by foreign governments, but by subnational groups, then who has the right to try and help them to achieve that security? Is it time to move beyond traditional concepts of national sovereignty and put the interest of people first? If so, how should such a policy be implemented?

The security of Sub-Saharan Africans is threatened by domestic governments and exacerbated by aggrieved sub national groups that perceive armed movements as a solution to re-establish the legitimacy of the state. As a result of these military coups and civil wars, new security threats, such as the trafficking of illicit arms and drugs, and human beings, have emerged in the region. This is so because in order to survive, a significant number of youths have engaged in these activities. Cooperation between Sub-Saharan African States to implement Human Security is not moving beyond rhetoric and discourse, and there is almost no implementation of this concept on the continent. This is due to the lack of interest on the part of governments, weak collaboration with civil society groups and a lack of financial resources. Effective implementation of Human Security in Africa must begin with Africans first, although other actors from the local to the international level should also participate if the process is to succeed.

Methodology

This paper is based on qualitative research, although some quantitative research has been used for the selection of African countries. I analyze how the most powerful countries in Sub-Saharan Africa attempted to influence the "weaker" states within the region to adopt a Human Security agenda. These countries were chosen on the basis of economic growth measured by the Gross Domestic Product, political participation and human rights, human development, economic opportunity and rule of law; this data was collected from the Ibrahim index that looks at the political, economic and social stability of countries in Sub-Saharan Africa. The data collection used included statistics from the UNCTAD (United Nations Conference for Trade and Development) website's ranking of countries by development. The countries with the highest scores in each sub region of sub-Saharan Africa notably South Africa in Southern Africa, Kenya in Eastern Africa and Ghana in Western Africa were chosen.

The analysis of the results found was mostly developed from a liberal perspective, since the concept of Human Security is mainly associated with this ideology. The main text used for the research was the edited book of Jamila Abubakar, Kenneth Ojeme and Habu Galadima called *Conflict of Securities: Reflections on State and Human Security*. This book was relevant to my research as it provided information about the root causes of Human Insecurities in Africa and direction on the implementation of this emerging concept in the region. For the foreign policies of the countries chosen, a number of sources, including scholarly journals and government documents, provided insight. Numerous scholarly journals gave information about various regional institutions such as the AU, ECOWAS and the SADC

Security agendas. These same articles offered solutions for better implementation of Human Security on the continent. However, there were limitations that hindered the acquisition of some data; little has as yet been written about the recent foreign policies of Ghana and Kenya.

Internal and external factors contributing to Human Insecurities in Sub-Saharan Africa

Human insecurities in Africa have their root in colonialism; during the 1885 Berlin Conference, the colonial powers created arbitrary borders that separated similar ethnic groups and combined different, often rival, groups. Hence the cultural identity that enabled these ethnic groups to co-exist was changed into a political identity where access to resources was limited between those considered "Settlers" and "Natives". This trend continued after independence, when rulers (Dictators) established Neo-Patrimonial/Clientelist regimes (Abubakar 66), and states' resources were used by rulers to gain loyalty of clients in order to maintain the ruler's powers. The first president of Cote d'Ivoire, Houphouet Boigny used this tool with Ivoirians and other African immigrants in order to maintain his power in the country (Abubakar,76).

Moreover, the Cold War politics between the United States and the Soviet Union had an effect on the instabilities in Sub-Saharan Africa (Adejumobi, 65). Each of the superpowers supported dictators to preserve their own interests . In Liberia, for example, from 1950-1980 a military government was established and was centered on the ruler (Adejumobi, 65). Thus, the US supported such regimes because they were considered "the main stronghold against the spread of communism in Africa". (Adejumobi, 66).

Furthermore, structural adjustment programs imposed by the Bretton Woods institutions such as the International Monetary Fund (IMF) and the World Bank, often exacerbated Human Insecurities in Africa (Abubakar,66-67). The State was to be less involved in the economy of the country. Economic inequalities based on increasing ethnic marginalization grew, and access to public goods were limited to the leaders and political elite's ethnic group. This factor caused further underdevelopment in the region.

This lack of economic development contributed to the growth of a number of militia. These sub national groups attempted to depose their current government, to supposedly improve the conditions of the African peoples. However, these rebel movements and militias often aggravated the conflicts, between and within states. Firstly, they attempted to gain power through military coups which often led to civil wars. For example in the Democratic Republic of Congo, Laurent Kabila overthrew President Mobutu in 1997 in a military coup, and declared himself president. Over the early years of his reign, he promised to move the country toward democracy; yet he would not tolerate any political opposition, often arresting individuals that opposed his policies. In addition, complaints about human right abuses by his forces persisted and the armed groups that aided him in overthrowing President Mobutu turned against him, mostly due to his favouritism towards his ethnic group[8]. Hence, the armed

---

[8] "[...] The Subsequent arrests of oppositionist, however undermined the apparent move towards democracy, and allegations of human rights abuses against Kabila's forces continued. In August 1998, the Banyamulenge, people of Tutsi origin who have helped bring Kabila to power launched an open rebellion in the eastern part of the country. Resentful of Kabila's

groups' political intentions to install better governance practices followed the trends they were attempting to change. Consequently, instability in the DRC and especially in the eastern part of the country still persists.

The civil wars in Africa had and continue to have a devastating impact on the continent. Transnational criminal activities such as trafficking of firearms and humans are becoming widespread. During the civil wars in Liberia and Sierra Leone, large numbers of firearms were smuggled into West Africa from Europe and other parts of Africa (Adejumobi,70); these were used by the Revolutionary United Front in Sierra Leone and the National Patriotic Front of Liberia. As a result, although the civil unrest has ended, these illegal firearms are still circulating in West Africa (Abubakar,67). They often get into the hands of belligerent groups in conflict zones (Addo, 204) and are used by youths to engage in criminal activities .

Similarly, human trafficking is increasing in West Africa (Addo,205). Children are trafficked across nations to work as child labourers or are and were used as soldiers during civil wars. The recruiters mostly target impoverished children and deceive their guardians by selling a dream of a better life (Addo,205). In the same way, women are also trafficked to other countries to be sexually exploited and often fall into the same deception.

How to address these security issues?

The concept of security has been mainly perceived through its realist conception, where the State is the referent and provider

---

seeming favouritism to members of his own ethnic group[...]"
(Encyclopedia Britannica Online, Laurent Kabila,2013).

of security. The main threats to security of the State are external such as other states or foreign sub-state actors, like Al-Qaeda or the Al-Shabaab in Somalia. The State must be economically developed and stable to deal with such issues militarily. However, it is evident that this conception of security does not apply to the continent of Africa. Human Security is the ideal approach to security in Africa (Abubakar 29).

"Human Security is intended to meet the needs of the most vulnerable individuals and groups by protecting Human Rights and promoting political inclusion, the environment, health, development and to alleviate poverty" (Abubakar,7-8). Some scholars argue that Human Security is best achieved by human emancipation which is the elimination of political, social and economic constraints that will keep the individuals from achieving what he or she will want to achieve (Abubakar,28). But at the same time, Human Security must not ignore economic development. For example, according to Robert McNamara "Security is development, and without development there is no security" (Mcnamara,149, found in Abubakar, 48). Economic development will undoubtedly contribute to the achievement of human security and keep political and social instabilities to a minimum. This means that citizens' economic, political and social needs are to be met. Thus Human Security depends on development, for one cannot be achieved without the other. So then, how is the continent and its various actors striving to implement this concept of Security?

Foreign Policy and Human Security

Cooperation between African states and institutions to implement Human Security is not moving beyond rhetoric and discourse. There is no effective implementation of this concept on the continent. This is due to multiple factors, notably the lack of interest of African states in the concept, weak collaboration with civil society actors and lack of financial resources. In southern Africa the governments have agreed to work together within the South African Development Community (SADC). South Africa is the region's most developed nation and it, along with Botswana and Mauritius, is trying to push this agenda forward, while other SADC countries are expressing a lack of interest in Human Security. Their governments are trying to keep local dictators in powers while also promoting their national economic interests.

Although South Africa and Botswana have sought to influence the SADC and its members to implement Human Security, it is facing challenges, because the region's conception of security is state centric, based on nationalism and independence due to the impact of colonialism and the apartheid regime. As a result, SADC countries are skeptical and fearful of any country that attempts to impose its norms to influence their domestic politics. These smaller States prefer a regional, SADC led, decision making and implementation of norms (Forsythe,265).

Most African States are skeptical about Human Security because the political elites believe it is a new idea imposed by western powers in order to maintain their colonial influence. For example, SADC countries believe that when South Africa and Botswana promote Human Security in the region they are being used as a tool by western powers. As a result, South Africa does not wish to appear hegemonic, knowing that its effort to push the Human Security agenda will be questioned and contested by weaker states in the region. Therefore, South Africa is constantly seeking multilateral consent from other states, before making any decisions. While this is a plausible democratic approach to decision making; at the same time, weak states in the region are reluctant to adopt a Human Security agenda in their domestic politics (Bischoff, 65), and seeking a multilateral consent will not drive these states to implement Human Security. Moreover, the cancellation of the SADC Human Rights Tribunal demonstrates to what extent State sovereignty is upheld over Human Security (Bischoff, 83). This tribunal was supposed to allow individuals to legally pursue member states in cases of human rights violations. But in 2012, during the SADC summit, it was decided that the tribunal should no longer be used by individuals, but by SADC states.

Similarly, Kenya is viewed as a country that is important in guaranteeing stability in the East African Region and as a promoter of Human Security in the region for its participation in the United Nations' and African Union's Peacekeeping initiatives (Bachmann, 126). It has undertaken actions toward Somalia and Somali immigrants in Kenya that affirm a different case. "Kenya is regarded as controversial due to its counterterrorism measures in Somalia and its involvement in the conflict of South Sudan" (Bachmann,132).

Since the aftermath of the tragedy of September 11 2001, the United States government primary security concern was the war against terrorism. The sub state actors that perpetrated these acts are the "Al-Qaida" networks, fundamental Islamists from the Middle East. Since east Africa has a large Muslim population, and it lies in proximity to the Middle East, the United States established the U.S Combatant Command for Africa also referred to as AFRICOM. This institution monitors terrorist activities in the region. It is a tool for the U.S to keep terrorism from spreading on the African continent (Abubakar,20). The Kenyan government receives funds from the United States to establish anti-terrorism institutions. These counter-terrorism programs have enabled the Human Rights abuses of certain Somalian Muslim populations considered suspect in Kenya (Bachmann, 138). For example, the Kenyan government and its security forces have been accused of committing extrajudicial killings (Bachmann,138) and of violating some international human rights conventions (Bachmann, 136) of Somalis suspected of being involved in the Kikambala terrorist attacks in 2002.

In addition, South Africa is not a follower of its own policies on Human Security. Post-Apartheid South Africa attempts to promote Human Security in the SADC region as well as the whole of Africa, but it has mostly been preoccupied with economic interests and trade (Forsythe, 265). Furthermore, there are principles that highlight its bilateral foreign policy: Sovereignty and protection of national interests, principles of equal treatment and universality where relations are maintained without consideration of religious or political orientation. The second principle means that South Africa is willing to maintain political and economic relationships with a country that is undemocratic and has a poor record of human rights protection. This can explain the reason behind South Africa's political and economic relations with African countries that have violated Human Rights. It is ironic to expect South Africa to focus on human rights, while at the same state it maintains political relationships with dictatorial regimes. In a declaratory sense, South Africa seems to promote Human Security due to the pressure exerted by its civil society groups (Forsythe,268). But in reality, economic interests are pursued first.

In the same way, Kenya is reputed as a regional peacemaker

on the continent, but it is also known for human rights violations which it claims are needed in order to keep terrorism from spreading on the African continent. In addition, economic interests rather than Human Security are most important to the country. During the Sudanese Civil war, Kenya was involved in the conflict through arms deals with South Sudan; they exported approximately 60 tanks to South Sudan (Bachmann, 132). In addition, Kenya was observed as silent during the Somalia conflict because it benefited from that conflict. It is rumored that the Somali piracy profits are later invested into the real estate sector in Kenya, which increases prices on Kenyan homes (Bachman 134).

The second factor that influences the lack of implementation of Human Security on the continent is the weak collaboration between African States and civil society. For example, the African Union Commission which is in charge of framing a Human Security agenda in Africa, attempts to include indigenous civil society groups and local actors into its discourse and implementation process. However, some AU member states such as Libya and Sudan have opposed the participation of these sub state groups in AU activities. In one instance, these two countries did not provide logistical or political support during the AU-Civil Society conference at the Sirte and Khartoum summit which were in their own territory (Tieku,34-35).

The third factor contributing to a lack of implementation of Human Security is the lack of financial resources. In West Africa, Ghana is making efforts to address transnational crimes in the region by signing various conventions created by ECOWAS. This same government lacks financial resources to train officials and acquire technologies in order to monitor its borders (Addo,206).

In the same way the CIDO (the African Citizens Directorate), which is an AU body charged with implementing the Human Security agenda, is understaffed and under-resourced. According to Tieku, only one person is hired as full time in this institution (Tieku, 34-35).

Recommendations for better implementation of Human Security

In order to implement Human Security in Africa, the root causes of human insecurities in Africa must be addressed. We cannot change the history of colonialism or Cold War politics in the region, but political and cultural norms framing the system of governance can be changed. These include Neo-patrimonial regimes linked to corruption which leads to poor access and distribution of state resources and undemocratic governance. The process of implementation must start with Africans first, starting from the sub state level with the role of the civil society, to the international level with financial and some logistical support from the United Nations. At the sub-state levels, indigenous civil society networks such as women's and student groups must mobilize and pressure the state, by calling for economic justice, good governance, democracy and the promotion of human rights. To achieve this end, there must be a foreign policy from below with a formation of transnational alliances (Abubakar, 28-29) between civil society groups from different African states. Similarly to the role played by indigenous civil society groups such as local chiefs and women's group in the peacebuilding process of Sierra Leone and Liberia after the civil wars, local groups should also play a role in transnational crime issues. The civil society networks should provide advocacy and research to the State and educate the population on the negative effects of these crimes (notably the illicit circulation of weapons and human trafficking in the region) (Adejumobi,73 and Addo,209).

Civil society networks should also be involved in the Moratorium on Small Arms Importation, Exportation and Manufacture in West Africa, which is an ECOWAS body charged with monitoring arms circulation in the region, in order to decrease the amount of weapons circulating on the region (Adejumobi,73). However most African countries do not have the ability to create the institutions that will be able to sustain civil society organizations (Abubakar, 29). How do we fix this? The United Nations can get involved in the implementation of Human Security by releasing funding to the African Union. The African Union can set clear standards on objectives to be met with implementation of Human Security and allocate these funds to sub regional organizations, which will then spread these funds to the civil society networks. But then, what is to be done in cases where states or regional organizations do not comply? To implement Human security at the State level, development and economic growth must continue to improve. This means the elimination of any barrier that might hinder the rate of economic development. Such barriers are civil strife or any form of political and social instability. To achieve this, the State and the governing elite must promote political participation and inclusion and install a democratic approach to governance. Clientelist regimes based on ethnic discrimination should be abandoned (Kotia, n.d., slide 16; Institute for Security Studies: Summary Report,3). The state should also adopt policies that will improve the well-being of their populations, with adequate healthcare programs, education and employment to keep youths occupied, since these youths could be recruited by belligerent groups during a civil war or might also engage in transnational crime activities. In addition, these African states, with the help of local groups and regional organizations should strictly monitor their borders. Regional organizations could be especially helpful in identifying government officials who are often engaged in these activities themselves. In addition, there should be a transnational court accessible to individuals, where citizens can pursue states in case of Human Rights violations. The SADC should re-establish the initial Human Rights Tribunal that was created to deal with such issues. The African Union should create a court that is the highest and supreme court of the continent of Africa. In a case where regional organizations are not able to effectively deal with prosecutions of states on human right violations, individuals could appeal to this supranational court. The African Union Court or the Commission on Human and People's right, can be the African Union bodies that will be in charge of such cases (Adejumobi, 76). At the International level, the United Nations and its development programme (UNDP) can monitor and finance Human Security initiatives and policy implementation in Africa. In the cases where African Institutions and states are not willing to address Human Insecurities in Africa, then the financial funds from the United Nations and the UNDP, can be slowly withdrawn, until the African states and institutions are serious about implementing this project by moving beyond discourse then the funds to finance such initiatives can be re-granted.

Sub-Saharan African individuals' securities are threatened by national governments and internal aggrieved sub-state groups rather than foreign governments. Therefore a Human Security agenda is needed in order to address these issues. African States must move from a realist conception of security to a human security centered approach. To implement this effectively, various actors must be included in the process, notably civil society groups, the national governments of African States, sub-regional and regional organizations, and at the international level, the United Nations, such as the United Nations Development programme. Implementing Human Security in Africa would prevent armed insurrections on the continent and will therefore lead to stability on the continent, because Human Security is national and regional security.

BIBLIOGRAPHY

Abubakar, J.J, Omeje,K, Galadima,H. (2010). *Conflict of Securities: Reflections on State and Human Security in Africa.* London: Adonis & Abbey Publishers Ltd.

Addo, Prosper Nii Nortey. (2008) Ghana`s Foreign Policy and transnational security challenges in West Africa. *Journal of Contemporary African Studies* **26** (2):197-211

Adejumobi, Said (2004). Conflict and Peacebuilding in West Africa: The role of civil society and the African Union. *Conflict, Security and Development* **4** (1): 59-77

A View from the Cave. Reporting on international aid and development. Governance: The Best and Worst Nations in Africa (2011). Retrieved from < http://www.aviewfromthecave.com/2011/10/governance-best-and-worst-nations-in.html>

Bachman, Jan (2012). Kenya and International Security: Enabling Globalisation,

Stabilising 'Stateness', and Deploying Enforcement. Gothenburg Centre of Globalization and Development **9**(1): 125-143

Bischoff, Paul-Henri (2012). What's been built in twenty years? SADC and Southern Africa's political and regional culture. *Strategic Review for Southern Africa* **34** (2): 63-91

Brown, K, Smallman, S. (2011). *Introduction to International and Global Studies.* University of North Carolina Press.

COT Institute for Safety, Security and Crisis Management: 2007. Notions of Security: Shifting Concepts and Perspectives. Transnational Terrorism. <http://www.transnationalterrorism.eu/tekst/publications/Notions%20of%20Security.pdf> (2013, October 5)

Curtis, Dzineza A , Gwinyayi A (2012*). Peacebuilding, Power and Politics in Africa.* Ohio University Press.

Forsythe, David P. (2000). *Human Rights and Comparative Foreign Policy.* United Nations University Press.

Institute for Security Studies (ISS) Public Seminar Series: SUMMARY REPORT: Human Security and Kenya's New Constitution. African Conflict Prevention Programme. < http://www.issafrica.org/uploads/10NovReport.pdf> (2013, November 14)

Kotia, Emmanuel. *Emerging Security Issues: Emerging Threats to National Security and Development in Africa.* Kennesaw State University, USA. < http://works.bepress.com/emmanuel_kotia/5/> (PowerPoint)

Laurent Kabila. *In Encyclopedia Britannica Online.* Retrieved from < http://www.britannica.com/EBchecked/topic/309264/Laurent-Kabila>

Tieku, Thomas. African Union promotion of Human Security in Africa. *African Security review* **16** (2):26-37

United Nations Office of the Special Adviser on Africa: Human Security in Africa.
<http://www.un.org/africa/osaa/reports/Human%20Security%20in%20Africa%20FINAL.pdf>

United Nations Conference on Trade and Development. *UN list of Least Developed Countries*. Retrieved from
<http://unctad.org/en/pages/ALDC/aldc.aspx>

Vreÿ, Francois (2009). The African Union: From a Security Culture to an Emergent Strategic Culture? *Strategic Review for Southern Africa* **31** (1): 19-40

ASPECTS OF US
FOREIGN POLICY

8. CLINTON AND SOMALIA

A CASE OF FOREIGN POLICY DECISION MAKING
By: Ashley Walcott

Timeline of Events

January 20, 1993

• Clinton's inauguration. He inherited President Bush's mission and had to make the decision whether or not to keep the troops in Somalia.

May 5, 1993

• The UN secretary General Boutros-Ghali had called a cease fire after successful preparatory meeting at Conference Centre of the Economic Commission for Africa - ECA headquarters in Addis Ababa which Aideed attended.
• Ambassador Bob Okley, the representative in Somalia claims success. Prepares for UNITAF to withdraw. Clinton delays UNITAF's withdrawal to May 4th.
• Clinton finally launches United Nations Operation in Somalia 2 (UNOSOM II) which was a task force composed of less men whose objective was to control arms and maintain the cease fire.

June 1993

• Ferah Aideed breaks the cease fire and his men are deemed responsible for the deaths of 24 UN troops.
• The objectives of the mission change to begin pursuing the Somali war-lord. Farah Aideed named Public Enemy No. 1 by U.S.
• Resolution 837 is establised by the U.N. to find all those responsible.

August 27, 1993

• Secretary of Defense Les Aspin said: "We went there to save a people, and we succeeded. We are staying there now to help those same people rebuild their nation." He added, "President Clinton has given us clear direction to stay the course with other nations to help Somalia" *Center for Strategic and International Studies, Washington, DC, News Release, Washington: Office of the Secretary of Defense, p. 5.*

October 3, 1993

• UH-60 Black Hawk helicopters were shot down (on September 25th, 1993).
• Culminating the search for Aideed there is a firefight in Mogadishu.
• Aideed's supporters were killed, but 18 American soldiers were killed, 80 wounded.
• Historic day that one helicopter pilot was captured and dragged through the streets of Mogadishu by Aideed's supporters.

October 7, 1993

• Clinton's Addresses the nation: "Today I have ordered 1,700 additional Army troops and 104 additional armored vehicles to Somalia to protect our troops and to complete our mission. I've also ordered an aircraft carrier and two amphibious groups with 3,600 combat Marines to be stationed offshore. These forces will be under American command"(President Clinton, October 7, 1993, Address at the White house).
• Cliton's decision, like Bush's, had a strict withdrawal date set (for March 31st, 1994), however Congressional pressure is argued to have played heavily on that decision.

The United States of America's entry into post- cold war humanitarianism began with one notable mission in Somalia. In the early 1990s President George H.W. Bush, as the leader of a newly "hegemonic state", was asked to supply military and economic support to the United Nations mission to end the civil-war in Somalia (Walt 2000:64). The result of the U.S.'s participation in this mission was a series of divergent approaches to foreign policy making that left the situation in Somalia a political nightmare for the U.S. Heavily blamed for their lack of experience in humanitarian intervention, the American public as well as the U.S. congress forced President Clinton to justify the U.S.'s presence in Somalia, causing a political nightmare for the president and his administration. President William 'Bill' Clinton's decision to intervene in Somalia ultimately affected humanitarian interventions by the U.S. for in a profoundly negative way. The administration had decided against American intervention in humanitarian crises such as the crisis in Rwanda in 1994 where delayed action resulted in a mass genocide (Carroll, 2004).

This paper examines the decision making of President Bill Clinton in regards to the intervention in Somalia; more specifically, his decision to aid the U.N. in its efforts in preserving peace in Somalia in the year 1993. The two decisions that will be examined in detail are, first, President Bill Clinton's formal decision to support former President George H.W. Bush's approval of sending American military troops in Somalia on May 5th, 1993, and secondly, President Bill Clinton's decision to send additional troops to Somalia on October 7th, 1993. The paper sets out to determine what factors influenced the Clinton administration's decisions as it set its course on foreign policy. The hypothesis proposed is that the combination of presidential inexperience in foreign policy, bureaucratic politics, and the intervening variable of the post-cold war climate explain the motivation toward humanitarianism, and assertive multilateralism (decision #1). To implement his foreign policy decision, Clinton's administration made a series of decisions that led to the sending of additional troops to Somalia which followed by an abrupt change in foreign policy decision making (decision #2). To understand President Clinton's actions at this time, this paper will outline the decision making process by using the collegial decision making model. This model allows for open discussion and the evaluation of a full range of options, both of which contribute to "better" policy outcomes (Mitchell 2010:632). As per Mitchell, "With the collegial style, the President seeks to develop a "team-like" atmosphere in which he seeks out a diversity of policy opinions from his advisors." (Mitchell 2010:634). This best characterizes Clinton's decision making because the foreign policies applied to Somalia were largely influenced by contextual and structural factors that contributed to his changing ideals. Mitchell notes that Clinton "has been described as being very difficult to pin down on policy because of his ability to change in response to new information (Mitchell 2010:637)." An important factor for the success of this model however, is that President Clinton had minimal interest in foreign policy. It is noted that, "the President did not attend many of the high-level interagency meetings on foreign policy, relying heavily upon his aides (David 2003:10)." This will help explain how, although foreign policy making was made in a 'team environment', it was exceptionally rudderless during the Somalia debacle.

Key actors will be examined to determine their contribution to Clinton's decision making process. Seven actors, or power centers played contributory roles: (1) President H.W. Bush, (2) President Clinton, (3) Clinton's administration (the main actors being: Secretary of State, Warren Christopher; Secretary of

Defense, Les Aspin; U.S. representative to the U.N. Madeleine Albright), (4) U.N. Secretary General Boutros Boutros Ghali, (5) Senators and members of the House (notably the speakers of the two houses) (6) Somalian clan leader Farah Aideed, (7) and select interest groups. An intervening variable in this analysis will be used to explain the relationships between the independent and dependent variables. The independent variable in this analysis will be the causes or inputs that influenced the decisions made. The dependant variable will be the final effects of the process, or the decision. All research done will consist of a combination of primary and secondary sources. These sources will lead to a conclusion as to whether the hypothesis is proved or disproved. This process of foreign policy decision making will be outlined in three stages: problem definition, option generation, and policy decision (as per Knecht 2010:40).

Problem Definition

In early 1991, Mohamed Siad Barre, the military dictator and President of Somalia was ousted from his political rule. Barre, who had ruled Somalia for two decades, was overthrown by a coalition of clan leaders that made up the many militia groups in Somalia. This event sparked a long and drawn out civil war in which the remaining clans battled for power of the state. The fighting resulted in a destabilization of the state's political, economic and social structures and killed tens of thousands of people, forced civilians from their homes and resulted in famine throughout much of the country (Di Prizio 2002:46). Soon with a steeply declining economy, looting and extortion of food became common practice (Di Prizio 2002:45). The famine and suffering of the Somali people garnered international attention and enticed a form of intervention. It is "estimated [that] 300,000 Somalis had already died of starvation during more than a year of civil war that followed the ouster of President Mohammed Siad Barre in 1991" (Lorch, 1994).

April 1992- December 1993

By mid-1992, rival militias were disrupting farming, and the distribution of food was problematic. Several humanitarian relief organizations deemed intervention too difficult, although the International Red Cross and Doctors without Borders aided civilians amongst the anarchy (Brune 1998:17). This situation is also said to have delayed the U.N.'s response to the crisis. In April, the U.N. initiated a humanitarian intervention in Somalia (UNOSOM I) to attempt to reconcile the fighting factions in the country (Crocker 1995: 4). U.N. officials sought negotiations with only two clan leaders: Mohamed Farah Aideed (United Somali Congress) and Ali Mahdi Mohammed. Obstinately U.N. envoy Mohamed Sahnoun wished to speak to all Somali clans and sub-clans, but was overruled (Brune 1998:18). The mission failed to pacify the clan leaders. On December 2nd, the U.S. led a United Nations Task Force (UNITAF) to mitigate the violence and aid the U.N.[9] For the mission, 28,000 U.S. troops were deployed with a strict mission to secure major air and sea ports, facilitate food distribution channels, and create a safe environment for the relief operation. President Bush's interest in the mission was minimal[10], the U.S involvement was purely for humanitarian

---

[9] On December 3rd the Security Council adopted, unanimously, its resolution 794 (1992), authorizing the use of "all necessary means to establish as soon as possible a secure environment for humanitarian relief operations in Somalia" (UNOSOM I Mandate).

[10] The U.S. and U.N. had different interpretations of the mission and what the U.N.S.C. resolution 794 "Secure environment" meant. Bush understood that it would create secure conditions that would "permit the feeding of starving Somali people", Boutros-Ghali sought "peaceful conditions for future aid as well as temporary protection" (Brune 1998:22).

reasons. The mission and its duration were to be quick and end by January 19th 1993, the day he was to leave office. Once that was accomplished, the military command would then be turned over to the United Nations (UNOSOM I Mandate document).

January 1993- March 1993

After Clinton's inauguration on January 20th, the U.S. had still not pulled out of Somalia. Clinton inherited Bush's decision and had to make the choice of whether or not to keep the troops in Somalia. On January 23rd, the UN Secretary General Boutros-Ghali called for a cease fire after successful preparatory meeting at the Conference Centre of the Economic Commission for Africa (ECA) headquarters in Addis Ababa[11]. In March, the conference was deemed successful by UNITAF officials, as noted by Ambassador Bob Oakley, the U.S. representative in Somalia who claimed a secure environment existed (Brune 1998:27). On March 26th, the U.N. Security Council adopted Resolution 814[12], largely because of American pressure to rehabilitate political and economic structures in Somalia (Bolton 1994:62). With this decision came the establishment of UNOSOM II. The mission objectives were to "take appropriate action, including enforcement measures, to establish throughout Somalia a secure environment for humanitarian assistance[...] to complete, through disarmament and reconciliation, the task begun by the Unified Task Force for the restoration of peace, stability, law and order (UNOSOM I Mandate)."

---

[11] On January 4 to 15th, 1993.

[12] In resolution 814 (1993), the Council also requested the Secretary-General, with assistance from all United Nations entities, offices and specialized agencies, to provide humanitarian and other assistance to the people of Somalia in rehabilitating their political institutions and economy and promoting political settlement and national reconciliation. The assistance included repatriation of refugees and displaced persons within Somalia, the reestablishment of national and regional institutions and civil administration in the entire country, the re-establishment of Somali police, and mine-clearance. (UNOSOM II Mandate)

May 1993- June 1993

Clinton delayed UNITAF's withdrawal until May 4[th,] 1993. On May, 5th President Clinton initiated the deployment of UNOSOM II in his address to the nation. The objectives of this mission were to build upon resolution 814 which was largely focused on nation building. The mission consisted of 14,000 troops for all of Somalia[13]. The U.S. had fewer army personnel, and troops included in this force, and the others were inexperienced and poorly equipped for the violent conditions in Somali (Brune 1998:28). For instance, the force included 1,500 nation building German engineers who were not trained for combat (Brune 1998:27). On June 4th, tensions between UNOSOM II officials and clan leader Aideed mounted. Special Representative of the Secretary-General, Admiral Jonathan Howe announced in June that UNOSOM II would enforce the Addis Ababa disarmament agreement and close down Radio Mogadishu. This decision backfired for the U.S., and only increased tensions between the two forces. On June 5th, the Somali militia believed to belong to General Aideed's faction launched a series of armed attacks against UNOSOM II troops throughout south Mogadishu (UNOSOM II Mandate). This involved the deaths of 24 Pakistani soldiers who were ambushed and killed. The U.S. and U.N. response was swift and quickly condemned Aideed for his involvement. The objectives of the UNOSOM II mission quickly changed to begin pursuing the Somali clan leader. The U.S. named Farah Aideed as Public Enemy No. 1 and focused its attention on this rather than the previous mandate of nation building. The U.N. also reacted, and adopted

---

[13]UNITAF had claimed responsibility for 40% of Somalia's territory (37,000 overall troops in southern and central Somalia). This is compared to the 14,000 overall troops responsible for all of Somalia (UNOSOM II Mandate). This number was raised to 28,000 in August (but consisted of inexperienced troops).

UNSC resolution 837[14] which promised to find all those responsible for the attacks.

August 1993- October 1993

On August 21st, General Colin Powell (as Chairman of the Joint Chiefs of Staff) obtained Secretary of Defense Les Aspin's consent to send 400 U.S. ranger and delta forces to search for Aideed (Cohen 2007:48). On August 27th, Aspin said "We went there to save a people, and we succeeded. We are staying there now to help those same people rebuild their nation" he added, "President Clinton has given us clear direction to stay the course with other nations to help Somalia (Aspin 1993)." Tensions in Somalia between the two sides were mounting, and on September 25th, two UH-60 Black Hawk helicopters were shot down. The search for Aideed culminated in a firefight in Mogadishu. On October 3rd, raids by the U.S. military killed 54 Somali's, 24 U.N. troops and 5 American soldiers killed, bringing the mission total to 16 (BBC Home, 1993). This day marked a serious loss for the American people when two soldiers were captured by Somali forces after the attacks and killed, their bodies dragged through the streets of Mogadishu by Somali National Alliance captained by Farrah Aideed. The event was broadcasted to American television screens through media outlets like CNN and CBS which fuelled public outrage. After the October 3rd conflict, President Clinton addressed the nation on the 7th and proposed to send additional troops to secure the mission and ensure a secure environment for

---

[14] Resolution 837 was carried out on June 6th. It strongly condemned the unprovoked armed attacks against UNOSOM II which "appear to have been part of a calculated and premeditated series of ceasefire violations to prevent by intimidation UNOSOM II from carrying out its mandate". It reaffirmed that the Secretary-General was authorized under resolution 814 to take all necessary measures against those responsible for the armed attacks and for publicly inciting them, including their arrest and detention for prosecution, trial and punishment. The Council requested him to investigate the incident, particularly on the role of the factional leaders involved (UNOSOM II Mandate).

existing troops. Clinton's decision, like Bush's, had a strict withdrawal date. However congressional pressure played heavily on this decision.

Option Generation

A number of decision making errors were made with the attempt to create policy to address the civil war and continuing conflict in Somalia. Clear policy objectives were not set, multilateral foreign-policy decision making (the U.N.) took a primary role, presidential leadership was not present, local and cultural intelligence was not consulted, divergent policies were established and congressional concerns were ignored. Together these factors led the course of events in Clinton's decision making as noted in his addresses to the nation on May 5th, and October 7th, 1993. The intervening variable identified in this process is the post- cold war climate. The independent variables identified are Clinton's lack of foreign policy experience and the bureaucratic politics that occurred as a result of multiple state objectives. The dependent variable identified is the resulting decisions that were made.

Independent variables

Clinton's Lack of Experience in Foreign Policy Making

During the first term of his presidency, Clinton's administration focused heavily on the domestic political strategy. Within the Clinton administration, Warren Christopher, Les Aspin, Madeleine Albright, and Anthony Lake helped form much of the government's priorities upon assuming office. All of these members (save Aspin) were veterans of the Carter administration and had worked together in some capacity before. They were Clinton's advisory team, and they all focused on the U.S. domestic situation. Most notable was the attention given to aid in the failing American economy, which included: unemployment, the runaway deficit, the health care crisis, and welfare reform (Clinton, 1993).

The collective stance on foreign policy however, was unclear. At the beginning of his presidency, Clinton avoided or neglected foreign affairs and no principles were formulated to guide the nation following the break-up of the Soviet Union (Henriksen 1996:11). Anthony Lake[15] was quoted in saying he had to, "keep foreign policy from becoming a problem –keep it off the screen and spare Clinton from getting embroiled as he went about his domestic business (McCormick 2010:154)". All members of Clinton's cabinet were said to be inexperienced in foreign policy making, which led to a collective, 'team build' environment in which policy was made retroactively, rather than proactively. Warren Christopher in a public address commented that, "When it is necessary, we will act unilaterally to protect our interests (Lewis 1993:20)."

By May, events in Somalia were prompting a more prominent U.S. role with the adoption of U.N. resolution 814. Now a nation building mission, the establishment of U.S. domestic economic interests seemed to stretch to the mission in Somalia. The proposed objective towards nation building was premature, and the U.S. could not pursue this aim amongst the anarchy in Somalia without a massive pacification campaign (Henriksen 1996:10). Clinton's lack of expertise meant that he had to rely heavily on his advisors, and Albright, noted for her work on human rights set forth a policy to help achieve both the U.S. and U.N. objectives (Cohen 2007:48).

The Clinton administration's first attempt to establish a

---

[15] Then Clinton's campaign foreign policy advisor

foreign policy was termed "assertive multilateralism". This policy would offer U.S. support while minimizing logistical input. Announced by Secretary of state Warren Christopher and Les Aspin, assertive multilateralism was a 'hands off' approach to foreign policy making[16] (Henrikson 1996:12). The move toward assertive multilateralism, which included American support for the world's organization's "peacekeeping" efforts, was the U.S.'s attempt to legitimize this new policy (Lewis 1993:14). Expressing American approval of this new direction, Albright was quoted in saying that, "[by moving from] feeding starving people to establishing security in the region... we will embark on an unprecedented enterprise aimed at nothing less than restoration of an entire country as a proud, functioning and viable member of the community of nations (Cohen 2007:48) ."

Conversely, the last minute decision to adopt this policy and the lack of military experience of Clinton's team caused a series of short sighted decisions during the mission in Somalia. With the U.S.'s involvement in Somalia, a critical factor in the failure of UNOSOM I's success and increasing tensions amongst U.S. troops and Somali clan leaders was the lack of understanding of the Somali clan based political culture (Stevenson 1993:142). The poor tactical organization was exposed in the administration's lack of success in pacifying Somali clan leaders, and the State Department's limited experience with U.N. peacekeeping. This meant that a primary understanding of the environment that they were trying to 'rebuild' was missing. Further, "the structural problem inherent in the Clinton administration's foreign policy apparatus ... [was] the lack of high-level attention and

---

[16] Following this decision Albright testified before a house committee on June 24th that assertive multilateralism did indeed serve US interests (Henriksen 1996:11).

coordination of U.S. African policies except when a crisis or domestic politics forces those policies to the top of the foreign policy agenda (Schraeder 1998:4)." The retroactive attention of the U.S. in Somalia failed to take into account important features of the state. As Stevenson remarks, "Somalis are 99 per cent Muslim and share common ethnic origins. So clans are not, for the most part, religiously or ethnically based. Instead they are vast patrilineal networks that originated generations ago (Stevenson 1993:142)." Further, as Clarke and Herbst state,

> The intervening forces failed to recognize which Somalis had been victims. Collapsed states like Somalia are often pictured as reverting to a Hobbesian state of nature, a battle of all versus all. Much of what appears to be incomprehensible warfare in Somalia is a struggle for land between the African farmers in the south and the northern, clan-based nomadic groups, which are better armed. (Clarke et al 1996:79)

The lack of clear foreign policy objectives early in the administration's first term led to a faulty process of decision making. The adoption of 'assertive multilateralism' set forth state objectives that were not shared by all actors involved. This form of collegial decision making formulated state objectives in foreign policy decisions in Somalia. However, these decisions did not employ any contextual knowledge of Somalia, nor did they involve presidential leadership.

Bureaucratic Politics

The U.S's goal's entering into the mission in Somalia was

humanitarian intervention with the use of force. This was amended to include nation building in March, and later in June assertive multilateralism was added to the mix. The lack of clear objectives for foreign policy in Somalia is what resulted in a mission creep that reflected pressure from the U.N. Secretary General Boutros Ghali for a stronger U.S role in the mission[17] (Bolton 63; Evans 29). Following the deployment of UNOSOM II the mission strategy did not change, even though the withdrawal of UN task force and UNOSOM I left less troops (14,000) and more areas of coverage. Military operatives were trained in combat, but they had no experience in the hostile climate they were thrust into.

Albright's 'assertive multilateralism' was intended to guide US foreign policy, and in June President Clinton moved to solidify the policy. Clinton instructed the National Security Council to draft Presidential Review Directive #13 (PRD-13)[18]. PRD-13 was the Clinton administration's review of policy on American participation in international peacekeeping activities. It redefined the term "national interest" to include a humanitarian threat abroad (PRD-13 Peacekeeping Operations, 1993). This is noted by Albright's key note address to the national war college on September 3, 1993. "The Clinton administration is fashioning a new framework that is more diverse and flexible than an old a framework that will advance American interests, promote American values, and preserve American leadership" (Albright

---

[17] Secretary General Boutros Ghali was quoted in saying, "such a force could obtain stability very quickly. I know Somalia. I have been there many times." His over confidence points out faulty decision making on the part of the U.N. (Bolton 1994:63).

[18] It is important to note that this directive was not ratified, but only drafted. It was also never released to the public, but obtained by the Washington post.

1993). This "new framework" was a clear indication that the country's objectives were changing. Despite congressional concerns, Clinton administration displayed their seriousness in pursuing force in concert with other means. Henriksen states that, "what transformed the Somali humanitarian mission from a narrowly defined success to a political debacle was the Clinton administration's determination to expand its endorsement of multinational, U.N.-sponsored peacekeeping operations while maintaining an independent command" (Henriksen 1996:10). This all changed when U.S. troops were attacked on June 5th. The American effort to carry out retribution for the lost American soldiers became a political red herring[19]. The decision making of the Clinton administration then fragmented between pursuing peacekeeping and capturing Aideed. While the State Department was emphasizing the need for political reconstruction and negotiated outcomes among all the various clan militia groups, the Pentagon was carrying out military operations designed to militarily defeat and capture militia leader Mohammed Farah Aideed (Schraeder 1998:4).

In late 1992 both the State Department and the Pentagon indicated their seriousness as participants in engaging peacekeeping, above and beyond being primary financial and logistical supporters (Mackinnon 1999:39). The Pentagon was not fully involved with the review process (of PRD-13) until July 1993 for a number of reasons, including the lack of knowledgeable staff and a general reluctance to get involved in what was considered to be largely a political exercise. Due to the Pentagon's limited direct experience with UN peacekeeping, there was a very small

---

[19] An idiom used to describe an event or person that misleads or distract from the main event or subject. In this context it is used to narrate the distraction that the American administration carried out by calling for an aggressive response to the attack on U.S. troops and pursuing the Somali clan leader Aideed (American enemy #1).

number of people in the Defense Department with any expertise in this area; in 1993 there were only seven people working on peacekeeping issues for the Joint Chiefs of staff (Mackinnon 1999:45). After the firefight in October, the State Department began distancing itself from the policy of 'assertive multilateralism' (Mackinnon 1999:38). Disapproval of the new foreign policy sent Clinton's team scrambling to re-establish the U.S.'s ever changing stance on foreign policy. Secretary of State Warren Christopher, made the point explicit, the US strategy would now be a purely diplomatic one, and that the State Department was hoping to enlist a number of African leaders, to help find an African solution to an *African problem* (Mackinnon 1999:38).

In Congress, senators such as James Carter and other U.S. congressional critics mandated a re-evaluation of U.S. policy (Krauss 1993). Congress began to stir, and Senate speaker Robert C. Byrd (D-W.Va.) called for the withdrawal of American forces, referring specifically to President Bush's plan for only a very brief American humanitarian mission (Krauss 1993). He also complained that the Administration had abdicated to the United Nations in the making of policy toward Somalia, calling it "a migration of responsibility" (Krauss 1993). Indeed it seemed that during the mission the Democrats were for the mission and the Republicans against. However after the events of October 3rd, unanimous disapproval surfaced. Senator John McCain was quoted as saying "the mission has been accomplished," on the Senate floor. He continued, "It is time to come home. Our mission in Somali was to feed a million starving [people] who needed to be fed. It was not an open-ended commitment. It was not a commission of nation building, not warlord hunting, or any of the other extraneous activities which we seem to have been engaged in" (C-Span, 1993). The distaste for the U.S.'s continued involvement in Somalia prompted Congress to pass a non-binding resolution on September 25 (PRD 25). This directive established that the President must obtain congressional approval if U.S. forces were to remain in Somalia after November 15, 1993. The lack of high-level coordination by the administration in the context of the post-U.S. firefight in Mogadishu influenced Clinton's decision to abandon nation building in his foreign policy making. Clinton's decision to remain in Somalia with a firm withdrawal date demonstrated his attempt to adapt to congressional opinion while maintaining his administrations collegial decision making.

Intervening variable

The Post-Cold War Climate

The collapse of the Soviet Union affected the U.S. in a favourable way. Prior to his inauguration, President Clinton proposed to re-define his foreign policy. In his candidacy Clinton argued "with the end of the cold war [...] American foreign policy must change to meet the challenges of the end of the twentieth century and to prepare for the twenty-first" (McCormick 2010:153). Needed for this new era was "a new vision and the strength to meet a new set of opportunities and threats" (McCormick 2010:153). Clinton claimed that a strong domestic economy would be his main foreign policy priority, since they are "two sides of the same coin," and vowed to join other countries to support emerging democracies around the world (Clinton 1992). McCormick states that, "domestic policy and foreign policy would be tied together because only by shoring up America's economic and social strength at home would the United States have an effective economic and security policy abroad " (McCormick 2010:154).

The removal of another major power meant that the U.S. was now in a position to lead the world. This security allowed for a broadening of U.S. roles, and would allow for the U.S. to pursue objectives that no other state would contemplate (Walt 2000:64). The post-cold war climate helped to determine what direction Clinton's foreign policy would take. However, upon assuming office, the administration was met with a new demand for U.S. power and strength. The undersecretary of State for Political Affairs, Peter Tarnoff, indicated to reporters that "the U.S expected to play a diminished world leadership role--in part because of the collapse of the Soviet empire and the manifest failures of Marxist ideology, but also in substantially larger measure because of pressing domestic economic difficulties[20] " (Lewis 1993:14) This was perhaps because "with a shrinking budget and reduced manpower, the military leadership has been compelled to operate at higher tempo, which, if the present trend continues, will provoke a decline in troop morale and recruitment problems, as well as a decline in wartime readiness of men and equipment" (Lewis 1993:20). The U.S. would no longer be expected to intervene in all of the world's political and economic upheavals, but according to Tarnoff, would "save" its power for "those situations which threaten our deepest national interest"(Lewis 1993:14). International involvement would be on the back burner until of course it brought in importance to U.S. national interests.

In regards to humanitarian intervention, "America's cold war world view typically depicted dependent states as having inferior militaries; backward, underdeveloped cultures; constant economic deficits; and political structures characterized by internal instability and inefficient policies" (McCoy 2000:39). The

---

[20] In May, 1993 referring to the Federal budget deficit as reported in the N.Y. Times

self-image of the American administration was at the time, "described ... in a superior fashion, using phrases such as "world leader," "superpower," "family of nations," "nurturing," "promoting" and "interests." (McCoy 2000:40)." Thus, the motivating factor for involvement in Somalia was less a political factor and more a moral imperative. In Clinton's words "The U.S. must continue to play its unique role of leadership in the world (McCoy 2000:40)." Also, in his address on October 7th when Clinton said that "only the U.S. could help stop one of the great human tragedies at this time" (Clinton 1993).

Policy Decision

Clinton's decision on May 5th to endorse a former policy on humanitarian intervention was irrational given his lack of military experience, knowledge of the situation in Somalia and his unclear stance on foreign policy. On October 7th in his address to the nation Clinton abandoned his previous attempt to solidify his administration's foreign policy initiatives, largely because of the bureaucratic and unpopular uproar that ensued after the firefight in Mogadishu and the loss of American soldiers' lives. The decisions made in the context of the post-cold war climate influenced Clinton. And the decision to intervene without a firm policy in place led to mismatched ideals. The anarchy in Somalia made any type of nation building difficult, a point was raised by Congress; yet Clinton and his administration did not take this into consideration in the decision making process. In fact, the evidence supplied indicates that *in spite* of congressional concerns, the President acted outside of collegial decision making to achieve his preferences.

In conclusion the hypothesis is proved, but is limiting.

Collegial decision making accounts for the collective disorganization of the Clinton administration concerning foreign policy and Somalia. It does not, however explain Clinton's resolution to carry out his own decision on October 7th to send additional troops to Somalia. The explanation delivered in his address that best summarizes the confusion in foreign policy making at the time is seen here,

> "This past weekend we all reacted with anger and horror as an armed Somali gang desecrated the bodies of our American soldiers and displayed a captured American pilot, all of them soldiers who were taking part in an international effort to end the starvation of the Somali people themselves. These tragic events raise hard questions about our effort in Somalia. Why are we still there? What are we trying to accomplish? How did a humanitarian mission turn violent? And when will our people come home?" (President Clinton, October 7, 1993, Address at the White house).

A possible explanation was the mission suffered from poor tactical and foreign policy decision making stemming from the contextual political climate of the U.S. at the time. The state's goals suffered from a mission creep that began with humanitarian, turned nation building, turned assertive multilateralism. It is claimed that "The Americans and the U.N. came in with a kind of arrogance," said a senior United Nations official… "Their psychological operations were naive, their intelligence very poor. They didn't speak the language. They met

with few Somalis. This has damaged the credibility of the U.N."
(Lorch, 1994). What is clear is that following the withdrawal of
U.S. forces from Somalia in March 1994, (at a total cost of 147
fatalities) these events continued to influence American foreign
policy making for years to come. The Rwandan genocide that
occurred years later in 1994, is argued to have been ignored by
President Clinton as the U.S.'s foreign policy making blunders had
so negatively affected them in the past (Rory, 2004). According to
American historian and human rights activist Alison Des Forges,
"They feared this word would generate public opinion which
would demand some sort of action and they didn't want to act"
(Rory, 2004).

BIBLIOGRAPHY

Albright, Madeleine K. (1993) Use Of Force In A Post-Cold War World.
    Address At The National War College, National Defense
    University, Fort McNair. Washington, DC.

Aspin, Les. (1993) Speech by Secretary of Defense Les Aspin to the
    Center for Strategic and International Studies. Washington, D.C.
    August 27.

BBC home. (1993) US forces killed in Somali gun battle. On this day 4
    October. Available at:
    http://news.bbc.co.uk/onthisday/hi/dates/stories/october/4/newsid_2
    486000/2486909.stm

Clinton, Bill. (October 7, 1993) Address on Somalia Miller Center:
    University of Virginia. Accessed: October 10 2013. Available at:
    http://millercenter.org/president/speeches/detail/4566

Clinton, Bill. (1993) Remarks on Operation Restore Hope. Miller
    Center: University of Virginia. May 5. Accessed: October 10 2013.
    Available at:
    <http://millercenter.org/president/speeches/detail/4564>

Clinton, Bill. (1992) Campaign speech. World affairs council. Aug. 13.

Bolton, John R. (1994) Wrong Turn in Somalia. *Foreign Affairs*. Feb.: 73- 1. pp. 56-66.

Bond, Jon R., Richard Fleisher. (1995) Clinton And Congress A First-Year Assessment. *American Politics Quarterly*. July: 23-3, 355-372.

Brune, Lester H. *The United States and Post-Cold war interventions: Bush, Clinton in Somalia, Haiti, and Bosnia 1992-1998*. Regina Books. 1998.

Carroll, Rory. US chose to ignore Rwandan genocide: Classified papers show Clinton was aware of 'final solution' to eliminate Tutsis. *The Guardian*. March 31 2004. http://www.theguardian.com/world/2004/mar/31/usa.rwanda

CBS report from Somalia 1993. Available at: http://www.youtube.com/watch?v=UMW8VSMZ5uY

Center for Strategic and International Studies: Washington, DC News Release. Office of the Secretary of Defense. p. 5.

Chester A. Crocker. (1995) The Lessons of Somalia: Not Everything Went Wrong. *Foreign Affairs*. Jun: Vol. 74, No. 3, pp. 2-8.

Clarke, Walter, Jeffrey Herbs. (1996) Somalia and the Future of Humanitarian Intervention. *Foreign Affairs*. Apr: 75- 2, pp. 70-85

CNN. Operation Restore Hope Air Assault. Available at: http://www.youtube.com/watch?v=PCYZOkaAUVk

Cohen, Jared. (2007) *One hundred days of silence: America and the Rwanda genocide*. Rowman and Littlefeild Publishers.

C-Span video library. U.N. Intervention in Somalia. Oct 14, 1993. Available at: http://www.c-spanvideo.org/johnmccain

David, Charles-Philippe. (2003) "Foreign Policy Is Not What I Came Here to Do" Dissecting Clinton's Foreign Policy-Making: A First Cut. Conference paper. June 26-28.

DiPrizio, Robert C. (2002) *Armed Humanitarians: U.S. Interventions from Northern Iraq to Kosovo*. JHU Press.

Evans, Ernest. (1996) The Clinton Administration and Peacemaking in Civil Conflicts. *World Affairs*. Summer: 159-1, pp. 24-28.

Friedman L., Thomas. (1993) The Somalia Mission; Clinton Sending More Troops To Somalia. *The New York Times*. October 07. Accessed: October 10 2013. Available at: <http://www.nytimes.com/1993/10/07/world/the-somalia-mission-clinton-sending-more-troops-to-somalia.html_>

George Bush. Somalia Invasion: "Doing God's Work". Available at: http://www.youtube.com/watch?v=tgCeFXeuE4U

Gertz, Bill. Aspin's decision on tanks was political; Report says he gave in to U.N.The Washington Times. Available at: http://www.netnomad.com/powell.html

Henriksen, Thomas H. (1996) *Clinton's Foreign Policy in Somalia, Bosnia, Haiti, and North Korea*. Hoover Press.

Hult, Karen M. (2000) Strengthening Presidential Decision-Making Capacity. *Presidential Studies Quarterly*. Mar: 30- 1. pp. 27-46

Kennan, George F. Somalia, Through a Glass Darkly. The New York Times. September 30, 1993. Available at: http://www.nytimes.com/1993/09/30/opinion/somalia-through-a-glass-darkly.html?pagewanted=all&src=pm

Klarevas, Louis J. (2000) Trends: The United States Peace Operation in Somalia. *The Public Opinion Quarterly*. Winter: 64-4 pp. 523-540.

Knecht, Thomas. (2010) Paying Attention To Foreign Affairs. How Public Opinion Affects Presidential Decision Making. University Park. *Pennsylvania State University Press*. Pp.203-233.

Krauss, Clifford. (1993) Mission In Somalia; High Cost for Clinton on Somalia Vote. The New York Times. Available at: http://www.nytimes.com/1993/10/16/world/mission-in-somalia-high-cost-for-clinton-on-somalia-vote.html

Lewis, William H. (1993). "Assertive Multilateralism": Rhetoric Vs. Reality. *Peacekeeping: The Way Ahead*, 13-28.

Logan, Carolyn J. (1996) U.S. Public Opinion And The Intervention In Somalia: Lessons For The Future Of Military humanitarian Interventions. *The Fletcher Forum of World Affairs*. Fall: 20-2.

Lorch, Donatella. (1994) Last of the U.S. Troops Leave Somalia; What Began as a Mission of Mercy Closes With Little Ceremony. The New York Times. March 26. Available at: http://www.nytimes.com/1994/03/26/world/last-us-troops-leave-somalia-what-began-mission-mercy-closes-with-little.html?pagewanted=all&src=pm

Mackinnon, Michael G. (1999) Rivals or Partners? Bureaucratic Politics and the Evolution of US Peacekeeping Policy. *International Peacekeeping*. London. Spring: 6-1. pp.32-54

Mccoy, Dorcas Eva. (2000) American Post-Cold War Images and Foreign Policy Preferences toward "Dependent" States: A Case Study of Somalia. *World Affairs*. Summer: 163-1. pp. 39-47

McCormick, James M. (2008) *American Foreign Policy and Process*. Cengage learning.

Menkhaus, Ken. (2008) International policies and politics in the humanitarian crisis in Somalia. Available at: http://www.odihpn.org/humanitarian-exchange-magazine/issue-40/international-policies-and-politics-in-the-humanitarian-crisis-in-somalia

Mermin, Jonathan. (1997) Television News and American Intervention in Somalia: The Myth of a Media-Driven Foreign Policy. *Political Science Quarterly*. Autumn: 112-3 pp. 385-403.

Mitchell, David. (2010) Does Context Matter? Advisory Systems and the Management of the Foreign Policy Decision-Making Process. *Presidential Studies Quarterly*. December: 40-4.

PRD-13 Peacekeeping Operations. Washington Post. Aug. 5, 1993 Available at: https://www.fas.org/irp/offdocs/pdd13.htm

Schraeder, Peter J. (1998) Guest Editor's Introduction: Trends and Transformation in the Clinton Administration's, Foreign Policy toward Africa (1993-1999). *A Journal of Opinion*. 26 -2. pp. 1-7

Schmitt, Eric. (1994) U.S. Weighs Withdrawal From Somalia. The New York Times. July 22. http://www.nytimes.com/1994/07/22/world/us-weighs-withdrawal-from-somalia.html

Shafitz, Jay, Chiristopher Borick. (2008) Introducing public policy. New York: Pearson Longmen. Pp. 62-72.

Stevenson, Jonathan. (1993) Hope Restored in Somalia? *Foreign Policy*. Summer: 91. pp. 138-154.

S J Res 45 - Authorization for Use of U.S. Armed Forces in Somalia – Key Vote. Project Vote smart. Available at: http://votesmart.org/bill/2732/#.UoCETnDryrE

UNOSOM II Mandate. UN Document. Available at: http://www.un.org/en/peacekeeping/missions/past/unosom2mandate.html

UNOSOM I Mandate. UN Document. Available at: http://www.un.org/en/peacekeeping/missions/past/unosom1backgr2.html

UN Security Council Resolution 794, Somalia. Council on Foreign relations. Available at: <http://www.cfr.org/somalia/un-security-council-resolution-794-somalia/p24237>

Urging Withdrawal Of American Troops From Somalia. (1993) House Of Representatives. Congressional Record 103rd Congress. Available at http://thomas.loc.gov/cgi-bin/query/z?r103:H06OC3-756:

Vuong, Quynh-Nhu. (2003) U.S. Peacekeeping and Nation-Building: The Evolution of Self-Interested Multilateralism. *Berkeley J. Int'l Law*. 21-804. Available at: http://scholarship.law.berkeley.edu/bjil/vol21/iss3/15

Walt. Stephen M. (2000) Two Cheers for Clinton's Foreign Policy. *Foreign Affairs*. Apr: 79-2. pp. 63-79.

Woods, Emira. (1997) Somalia. For many in the U.S., Somalia is viewed as a powerful symbol of United Nations peacekeeping failure. Available at: <http://fpif.org/somalia/>

9. USA AND TAIWAN: DEMOCRACY AND THE TAIWAN RELATIONS ACT

A NEO- GRAMSCIAN UNDERSTANDING
By: Saquib Ahsan

American policies towards the Taiwanese state and the People's Republic of China are Janus-like. In regards to the US, there are attempts made to foster diplomatic/political/economic and cultural relationships with both [self-proclaimed] Chinese governments while also attempting to justify the American relationships with and against the two respective governments. In regards to Taiwan in particular, US officials have taken on a unique approach to maintain and develop this relationship with the former Republic of China (ROC). This paper explores the unique approach to international relations by the US and in doing so attempts to formulate a critique of US hegemonic behaviour toward the Taiwanese state. This paper suggests traditional neo-realist notions of hegemony are inadequate as they reduce power-relations between states to simple discrepancies of physical capacity and as such, they are inadequate in explaining the complex relationships between Taiwan and the US as well as relationships between other states. This paper will attempt to deconstruct and refute neo-realist notions of hegemony through an application of a neo-Gramscian model of hegemony. It will attempt to argue that the continual (quasi)-recognition of Taiwan's government by the U.S as well as the construction of various institutions (specifically the American Institute in Taiwan) is a prime example of 'cultural hegemony' in the international context.

Introduction – The Father of the Republic

During the early 20th century, Chinese revolutionary and 'founding father' of the Republic of China - Sun Yat-sen developed a political philosophy of government, one that he hoped would one day become the founding ideology of a Chinese republican government (Yat-sen, 1924). Sun's political philosophy relied on three major principles which he believed were the foundations of an all-powerful government. Translated into the 'three principles of the people' (from Mandarin Chinese to English) the principles of Minzu (nationalism), Minquan (democracy) and Minsheng (people's livelihood) were to be the defining feature of the Republic of China and the basis of its governmental system.[21] So much so that the first line in the Republic of China's national anthem is a direct reference to the three principles. Sun argued to great lengths that "equilibrium between the popular power and governing efficiency is essential in securing political progress" (Sun Yat-sen: 1924, 111). He was also a firm supporter of self-determination, arguing that the people ought to have the right to self-determination and absolute control over their governments so that "autocracy and exploitation would give way to democracy and liberty" (Sun Yat-sen: 1924, 111). Sun had also attempted to move closer to a 'Western' style of government through arguing that constitutionalism and division of power within the government (see; Yat-sen five-power constitution theory) will enhance not only the control of a government, but also its duty. In short, when one reads his book 'The Three Principles of The People', one will find that a good portion of his arguments are those in favour of constructing a new Chinese state mainly based upon seemingly Western principles.

---

[21] It is important to note that while the ROC had made 'attempts' to democratize, it had remained an authoritarian state for much of the Cold War

While the principle of people's livelihood may be seen as a socialistic one, it is clear that based on Sun's three principles, much of the early Taiwanese governmental philosophy shared components to the "Western" model of government – which was largely a democratic one. This does not mean however that since The Republic of China's inception, it has been working closely with the US. In fact it the opposite is true; during the early 20th century, non-interventionist doctrines as well as anti-imperialism were at the centre of US foreign policy and decision-making; leading to a an isolationist American policy in regards to international affairs (Harrington: 1937). In addition, China on the other hand, promoted nationalism in an attempt to "stand up" to Manchurian society as well as other Chinese 'sub-groups', the Japanese and Western influence by constructing and reinforcing a national Chinese 'image' over particular 'ethnic' ones (Sun Yat-sen: 1924, 12). However since the Republic was dedicated to specific Western principles such as the concept of democracy, not only did this mean that Western principles would go on to define the core political aspirations of the Republic, but also that it [the Republic] had dedicated much of its political will to a Western style constitutional government, one that would be compatible with the Western order.

Neo-Realism and 'Hegemony'

This paper attempts to formulate a critique of US foreign policy through a neo-Gramscian interpretation of hegemony. In order to do so however, the traditional notions of neo-realist hegemony must first be challenged. Neo-realism or 'structural' realism is a school of thought which emphasizes the idea that conflict and mistrust among states is the end result of the existing, inherently anarchical international realm (Mearsheimer: 2006, 73). While much can be said about the inadequacies of neo-realism in regards to its hegemonic and power-relations theory; this paper will only explore two major interconnecting ones: the oversimplification and as well as the reduction of state power-relations and hierarchies to relations determined by a state's physical capacity. Structural realists like John Mearsheimer [offensive realist] interpret hegemony as simply 'power seeking' and he argues that all states seek to enhance their physical capacity in an attempt to secure themselves within the anarchical international system.[22] Other structural realists like Stephen Walt and Kenneth Waltz [defensive realists] however, argue that hegemony and security are sought out not through power seeking as such, but rather defense seeking through securitization projections and that such projects will inevitably and inadvertently prompt other states to take defensive initiatives for fear of the actual need one day to utilize said defensive capacities. (Walt: 1998)

While both structural realist theories may do well in explaining Cold War era 'strategic thinking' they ultimately oversimplify power-relations by reducing them to simple relations of military might. In the words of Mearsheimer "Realists believe that power is the currency of international politics." (Mearsheimer: 2006, 72). In addition, because neo-realists oversimplify power-relations they disregard and/or downplay issues of class and structural inequality within the international system. Since the neo-realist notion of hierarchy is understood through physical capacity, there is a disregarding of not only historical processes, but also the unequal formations and

---

[22] Mearsheimer , J . "Realism and the Rise of China." Lecture, John J. Mearsheimer speaking on the Rise of China and Offensive Realism from Koç University, Istanbul, October 10, 2012.

developments of states. Neo-realists do not account for injustices such as genocide, slavery and economic and political dispossession as factors that have influenced and to a large degree shaped the current status of the international system. It is also worthy to note that neo-realists do not include state-sanctioned violence and cross-continental systems of oppression (such as colonialism and imperialism) within their theoretical framework. In addition, the acceptance of the idea that sovereign states are the only actors within the international system in itself fails to explain the actual relationship between the sovereign state of the United States of America and the 'unofficial' sovereign state of The Republic of China. These concepts do not fit into the neo-realist model which itself is an ahistorical approach to international relations.

Neo-Gramscianism

In the early 1980s, York University academic Robert Cox had inadvertently developed a new theoretical model of international relations. Through recycling ideas from several theorists, particularly Italian socialist and political philosopher Antonio Gramsci's theories of state hegemony within capitalist societies, Cox developed a new critical theory of international relations (Cox: 1983). In addition to being a Critical neo-Marxist theory, neo-Gramscian theory redefined several traditional neo-realist terms such as 'hegemony', 'status quo' and 'power' through attaching political-economic, social and culture components and by placing a greater emphasis on institutional and cultural hegemony rather than simply physical capacity. Neo-Gramscian hegemonic theory can be summarized with a quote from Cox:

> Within a world order, a situation of hegemony may prevail 'based on a coherent conjunction or fit between a configuration of material power, the prevalent collective image of world order (including certain norms) and a set of institutions which administer the order with a certain semblance of universality (Cox 1981: 139)

The neo-Gramscian model of hegemony differs from the structural realist models of hegemony which place the 'anarchical' nature of the international system at the centre of states' pursuit of their national interests as well as the classical realist models that base the international system on the more ambiguous notion of 'human nature'. Neo-Gramscians generally emphasize the reinforcement of existing historical economic 'blocs' and institutions through coercive policies as the main source of conflict within the international system. According to Cox, institutional economic or 'historical' blocs (which are essentially a hierarchical class structure characterized by the juxtaposition of economic, political, ethnical and ideological spheres of activity) can only be established when a dominant hegemonic social class in a country, or in the case of the broader international system - a hegemonic state, maintains cohesion and identity in the bloc through the "propagation of a common culture" (Cox: 1983, 168). Neo-Gramscian hegemony puts less emphasis on a state's military capacity than on its ability to maintain regional hegemony through either reinforcing existing historical hierarchical economic and social blocs, or by formulating new ones (Cox: 1983).

Democracy and Political Culture

It is here that the theoretical critique of neo-realism through the lens of a neo-Gramscian framework will attempt to converge in an attempt to conceptualise the U.S – Taiwan relationship. Since neo-realism fails to acknowledge institutional structures other than military ones, it disregards the existence of not only the liberal international order, but also political cultures of nation-states which this paper argues are imperative to understanding US foreign policy discourse with respect to Taiwan. This paper maintains that neo-Gramscian concepts of hegemony are complex and more suitable for the analysis of the U.S – Taiwan relationship than traditional realist models as it emphasizes the conjunction of material systems of power with the prevailing political cultures and institutions designed to administer and maintain existing orders. Furthermore, there are many within the study of international relations who stress the vital role of democracy in resolving world conflicts, and while there are valid critiques of this democratic peace theory, it is true that the Taiwanese-U.S relationship is the direct result of an emphasis towards democratic institutions. While correlation may not entirely equal causation, there might indeed be some truth to this – that democracy in a sense connects states and governments that otherwise would have not formed alliances – politically, economically and culturally.

This paper will not attempt to push the boundaries of liberal democratic peace theory, but rather suggests that democracy and conformity to the Western model of government is in fact imperative to understanding U.S foreign policy with respect to the Taiwanese state. In other words, because Taiwan shows signs of conformity to the Western international system,

U.S policymakers will inadvertently and as well as consciously make an effort to preserving a democratic political ally. While the argument that political culture as a consolidator between sovereign entities across the world may not convince many firm believers of self-preservation and power-seeking as the ultimate incentives for state-interactions, the fact is that states often emphasize mutual understandings and shared cultures when building relationships, organizations or alliances (for example, NATO). It is important to understand what is achieved when leaders emphasize mutually-shared political cultures. To better conceptualise the importance of democracy in defining political relationships, one can turn to Roxanne Doty's examples of binary oppositions.[23] Doty argues that meanings are dependent on binary oppositions within the international system and that "the specific content of these oppositions indicates the dimensions along which the construction of subjects takes place" (Doty: 1993:312). In simpler terms, binary oppositions give meaning to concepts (ideas, beliefs, culture) and are simultaneously positioned against other concepts to reinforce their meanings. Doty's examples relate specifically to US imperialism within the Philippines. However the same analysis can be applied to US policy-discourse on Taiwan. Doty raises the concept of core oppositions which guided American policy toward the Philippines – 'Reason and Passion'. She argues that many Americans used the supposition that Western political thought was based on reason whereas Asiatic political thought was based on passion and emotion as a justification for an imperialistic policy toward the Philippines.

The U.S and Taiwan may not share the same 'reason'

---

[23] Binary Oppositions is not a concept exclusive to Doty or any particular international relations theory

against 'passion' opposition as both states mainstream political cultures and thoughts that do resemble each other to some extent. However according to Øystein Tunsjø, the binary oppositions of basic conceptions of 'good' and 'evil' can be applied to understand US policy discourse on Taiwan (Tunsjø: 2008). In his book *US Taiwan Policy: Constructing the Triangle*, Tunsjø borrows Doty's binary opposition argument as well her argument on the use of the basic conceptions of good and evil to construct 'images' of two 'opposing' and conflicting sides and argues that US Taiwanese policy discourse and narrative is constructed out of binary oppositions between good 'democratic states' such as Taiwan and bad 'authoritarian' states such as China (Tunsjø: 2008: 90). For Tunsjø this opposition between 'good' and 'evil' is important for US policymakers because it serves as an element for constructing Taiwan and China as two distinct kinds of subjects, further emphasizing and reinforcing the rhetoric of 'free loving Taiwanese people' being 'threatened' by Chinese Communists.

How do binary oppositions fit into the neo-Gramscian model? Culturally of course! If the connection between neo-Gramscian cultural hegemony and binary oppositions remains unclear then it is worth noting that it is through the construction of binary oppositions that people, groups and states can build and develop meaning within their relationship. In a sense, this meaning requires an emphasis or exaggeration of the 'other' or 'alien' within the international system. With a bit of imagination, one could even make a connection to fascist doctrines which attempted to consolidate political societies through the fabrication of 'the other'. In the words of political theorist and prominent Nazi supporter Carl Schmitt,

> The political enemy need not be
> morally evil or aesthetically ugly; he need not
> appear as an economic competitor, and it may
> even be advantageous to engage with him in
> business; and it is sufficient for his nature that
> he is, in a specially intense way, existentially
> something different and alien, so that in the
> extreme case conflicts with him are possible.
> (Schmitt: 1932: 27)

Ultimately while the PRC may have achieved a major foreign policy goal when it received official political recognition through the One China Policy, and while it may be that the US and many other states have gradually formed or maintained relations with the PRC for various geopolitical, military, strategic and economic purposes – it is through the propagation of the Taiwan Relations Act that the US demonstrates its dedication to preserving the interests of Taiwan in the presence of any threat from the PRC. In this scenario it becomes clear that the U.S considers the PRC an 'other'.

Taiwan Relations Act - The Unsinkable Aircraft Carrier

At the height of the Cold War during the 1960s, the PRC experienced a falling out with the Soviet Union. On December 15, 1978, President Carter announced that as of January 1, 1979, the U.S would end its diplomatic relationship with the ROC and instead recognize the PRC as the sole legitimate Chinese state. This was not entirely unexpected as since President Richard Nixon's secret visit to the PRC in 1972, there had been several attempts at reconciling relations with the communist state – most notably through the signing of the 1972 Shanghai Communiqué. When the US recognized the PRC as the sole heir to all of China, the Carter administration had produced an act that aimed to continue relations with the PRC while maintaining a separate relation with the Taiwanese state. Conservative think tank (the Heritage Foundation) political analyst and writer Stephen J. Yates observes,

> Members of the Senate Foreign Relations Committee expressed concern over the haste with which the Administration had moved late in 1978, as well as with the lack of consultation with Congress and the lack of adequate consultation between the United States and its allies. The committee's report pointedly noted that the bill as submitted by the Administration contained no reference to the interests of United States in Taiwan's security, and lacked any reference to the sale of defensive arms to Taiwan (Yates: 1999)

As a result Republican members of Congress found it necessary to not only re-evaluate the initial Taiwan Relations Act (TRA), but also the US relationship with the ROC in an attempt to clarify the United States' position on the Two China issue. Congress had been firm on its decision to maintain arm sales to Taiwan, arguing that it was in the interests of the US to do so. In the end, Congress won the battle with the Carter Administration, and the TRA in its current form today remains an embodiment of the conservative ideals represented by Congress in 1979. The language of the TRA is however ambiguous, and its legal justifications even more so. On one hand there is a recognition of the legitimacy of the One China Policy in favour of the PRC while on the other there is a no recognition of the legitimacy of the

PRC's sovereignty claims over Taiwan. There are also attempts to superimpose US interests in peace and stability as global interests. What is most bizarre about the Act is that it poses Taiwanese sovereignty as a human rights issue and that because America is dedicated to maintaining human rights, one of its primary objectives in regards to Taiwan will be to preserve the rights of its population.[24] The TRA continues to exist today as a contradictory piece of foreign policy legislation which governs U.S policy discourse on Taiwan. It is also an expression of the hegemonic ambitions of US foreign policy, and the methods by which it was implemented constitute a direct contradiction of the traditional forms of international relations. Since Taiwan was no longer a legitimate sovereign nation-state in the view of the world's leading hegemon and since the TRA proposed an abandonment of official political ties with Taiwan in favour for 'economic' and 'cultural' ones, the TRA as an instrument of foreign policy could not be implemented through direct political relations, but rather through some sort of international mediators. These 'mediators' emerged and manifested in the form of non-profit organizations and private corporations – particularly the American Institute in Taiwan (AIT).

American Institute in Taiwan

As a private corporate institution, the AIT's role within the international system is simple: serve in the interests of the US government and maintain unofficial ties with the Taiwanese government. The AIT functions like an embassy. It supports US citizens living in Taiwan with not only visa issues, but also in the traditional bureaucratic sense such as providing resources, information and news (via its website), and handling the

---

[24] See the Taiwan Relations Act. (1979). Public Law. U.S Congress.

paperwork relating to the deaths and births of American citizens in Taiwan. There is however a cultural aspect to AIT. Through a cultural outreach program which emphasizes the similarities between Taiwan and the US, the AIT attempts to reach out to local Taiwanese through highlighting the 'diversity of the United States'.[25] The cultural outreach program also provides scholarships and grants to American students studying in Taiwan and as well as Taiwanese students studying in America. Since the U.S has sworn off any 'official political' relations, the AIT is also responsible for promoting business and maintaining economic reports. To quote the AIT,

> AIT's Taipei Office (AIT/T) with a total staff of over 450 people undertakes a wide range of activities representing U.S. interests, including commercial services, agricultural sales, consular services and cultural exchanges. The Institute also operates a Chinese language school, trade center, and library. AIT has a branch office in Kaohsiung (AIT/K) that handles local commercial promotion, consular services, information and cultural work. (American Institute in Taiwan: 2014)

At first glance the AIT's task appears to be mundane and quite ordinary. What makes this institution an example of hegemonic behaviour? How would a neo-Gramscian analysis even apply to such a scenario? To answer to these legitimate questions, one must recognize that the American Institute itself serves as an example of US hegemonic behaviour. At its core, the AIT is a

---

[25] See American Institute in Taiwan. Cultural Programs.
http://www.ait.org.tw/en/arts-and-cultural-programs.html

constructed institution which exists through the juxtaposition of contradicting and conflicting interests. The institution serves as the mediator between the U.S and the 'unofficial' state of Taiwan and attempts to justify its existence through policy reference and cultural parallels. If old cliché analogies were accepted within the study of international relations, then the U.S policy discourse in regards to the Taiwan Relations Act is an example of the U.S 'having its cake and eating it too'.

Conclusion

In this last segment of the paper, the effectiveness of the Taiwan Relations Act is challenged. This paper does not utilize a particular theoretical framework to conceptualise on what level 'effectiveness' is understood, but rather it argues that the TRA has been largely successful in what it aims to accomplish. It is clear that the TRA has facilitated the survival of the Taiwanese "state". While the majority of the world's governments no longer recognize Taiwan as a sovereign state, its government and institutions are intact. Its population enjoys relative peace and commercial success and as well as relatively high standards of living. In this sense we can argue that the TRA is a success as it has facilitated the continuing existence of a democratic state. In the words of Jaw-ling Joanne Chang,

> The TRA provided a legal framework for the continuation of relations between the United States and Taiwan, and has stood the test of time. Trade between the two countries has grown spectacularly over the last twenty years, from $9.2 billion in 1979 to $51.2 billion by 1998. Taiwan is now America's seventh-largest trading partner. In 1998 Taiwan

imported $18.15 billion in American goods and services; the PRC, by contrast, only imported $14.25 billion. Cultural relations between the United States and Taiwan have also deepened significantly (Chang: 2000: 64)

Furthermore, there has been a gradual liberalization of Taiwanese political society since the enacting of the TRA. As Chang further notes, Taiwan's record on human rights has improved rapidly since the mid-1980s, martial law has been lifted since 1987, Taiwanese citizens can now travel freely to mainland China, restrictions placed on newspaper publishing have been lifted and of course, citizens can now participate in democratic elections. The success story of the TRA is almost self-evident.

This paper however does not take a normative stance in regards to the TRA; nor does it argue that the TRA was the 'right thing to do' or that conforming to the liberal model of 'Western' development is what all states 'ought' to strive for. Instead this paper asserts that the TRA is an example of a cultural hegemonic act by the US. In this respect, how successful the TRA has been is arguably irrelevant as its implementation signifies an attempt to foster political-economic unity – the results do not matter as much when discussing the action itself. Under a neo-Gramscian lens, both the Taiwan Relations Act and the American Institute serve as relatively successful examples of U.S hegemony and attempts to "propagate" and reinforce a "common culture" within the East Asian region. These policies and institutes act as justifications for U.S foreign policy towards Taiwan on an international level and more importantly allow the U.S to continue its relationship with the People's Republic of China. Without these institutions and policies, it can be argued that the

PRC and U.S relations would be filled with tension to say the least. The existence of these institutions allows the U.S to engage the region with more diplomacy – giving some legitimacy towards U.S interests overall. On the surface of international politics, it enables the U.S to appear democratic, less hegemonic and unoppressive. While tensions may arguably be high at times, it must be noted that the U.S's relationship with the PRC remains relatively strong in terms of political-economic integration (on an international level). The existence of these institutions and policies as this paper had attempted to argue, can be attributed to this deep economic connection between the two states.

BIBLIOGRAPHY

Bary, T. Lufrano, R. (2000). Sources of Chinese Tradition: From 1600 Through the Twentieth Century. Columbia University Press. 2nd ed

Cox, R. (1981) Social Forces, States and World Orders: Beyond International Relations Theory. Millennium Journal of International Studies

Chang Joanne J.J. (2000). Lessons from the Taiwan Relations Act. Orbis.

Cox, R. (1981) Social Forces, States and World Orders: Beyond International Relations Theory. Millennium Journal of International Studies

Cox, R. (1983) Gramsci, Hegemony and International Relations: An Essay in Method. Millennium Journal of International Studies

Doty, R. (1993). Foreign Policy as Social Construction: A Post-Positivist Analysis of U.S. Counterinsurgency. International Studies Quarterly, Vol. 37.

Dr. Yat-sen, S. (1924). The Three Principles of the People.

Harrington H. Fred. (1937) Literary Aspects of American Anti-Imperialism: 1898 – 1902. New England Quarterly. Vol 10.

Mearsheimer, J. (2005) "The Rise of China Will Not Be Peaceful at All." The Australian

Mearsheimer, J. Dunne, T. Kurki, M. Smith, S. (2006). Chapter 4 'Structural Realism'. International Relations Theories. Oxford University Press.

Peters, G. Woolley, T. J. (1979) *Jimmy Carter: "Taiwan Relations Act Statement on Signing H.R. 2479 Into Law. The American Presidency Project.* www.presidency.ucsb.edu/ws/?pid=32177

Schmitt, C. (1932). Der Begriff des Politischen. Rutgers University Press

Sharman, L. (1934) Sun Yat-Sen; His Life and Its Meaning; A Critical Biography. Stanford University Press

Tunsjø. Ø. (2008). Chapter 4 'Contemporary Challenges in US Taiwan Policy'.US Taiwan Policy: Constructing the Triangle (Asian Security Studies). Routledge.

Walt, Stephen M. (1998). "International Relations: One World, Many Theories." Foreign Policy.

Yates, J.S. (1999). The Taiwan Relations Act After 20 Years: Keys to Past and Future Success. The Heritage Foundation

10. US FOREIGN POLICY IN LATIN AMERICA

AN INTERPRETATION FROM THE BUSH TO THE OBAMA DOCTRINE
By: Saquib Ahsan

The foreign policies of the two most recent presidents of the United States of America in regards to Latin American have often been considered contradictory. Whereas President George W. Bush Jr. engaged the rising Latin American Left [Pink Tide] with opposition and hostility, President Barack Obama has attempted to shift away from blatant political opposition to building mutual trust and cooperation by promoting economic and security agreements through an increased emphasis on diplomacy. Obama's policies of cooperation when viewed critically however reveal a continuation with those of Bush's hard power strategy. This paper will attempt to apply a neo-Gramscian interpretation of the ideological shift within the political economy of Latin America in an attempt to conceptualize the shift in foreign policy between the two presidents. This paper maintains that the ideological differences of Bush and Obama are largely irrelevant with respect to their foreign policies in Latin America; while the Obama Doctrine and Bush Doctrines diverge as two opposing doctrines in some aspects, the two unexpectedly converge as they ultimately attempt to reassert historical U.S hegemony within the Americas.

The Bush Doctrine – A Brief Overview

While many may claim that Latin America had become an uninteresting region within Bush's foreign policy agenda (post September, 9th 2001), there is evidence which suggests that the

Bush Administration had applied many of the same principles and policies it had promoted and implemented in dealing with the perceived threats to national security from the Western Asia region toward several Latin American countries. There are a few fundamental principles and characteristics which have often been used to define and explain the Bush Doctrine: the notion of (i) unilateralism and (ii) democratization are two that will be assessed and critiqued within this paper.

Neo-conservatism is a term that has often been applied to the Bush Administration's foreign policy agenda; however as Stefan Halper and Jonathan Clark argue;

> [Neo-conservatives] Disdain conventional diplomatic agencies such as the State Department and conventional country-specific, realist, and pragmatic analysis. They are hostile toward non-military multilateral institutions and instinctively antagonistic toward international treaties and agreements. "Global unilateralism is their watchword. They are fortified by international criticism, believing that it confirms American virtue. (Halper; Clark: 2004:11)

The very notion of neo-conservatism promotes the idea of unilateralism; however unlike traditional realist notions of hegemonic unilateralism, neo-conservatives insist that it is America's inherent right and duty to spread its values and principles as well as act as a sort of lighthouse to the rest of humanity by any means, including coercive and military action if necessary. Neo-conservatism complements or reinforces the notion of unilateralism while also providing justifications for unilateral policymaking and diplomacy. The notion of unilateralism is most apparent in Bush's unwillingness and refusal to operate within multilateral institutions and agreements; the most well-known example would be the disregarding of the United Nations General Assembly's judgment regarding the invasion of Iraq in 2003. Other examples include Bush's withdrawal from the historic Anti-Ballistic Missile Treaty which was signed by the U.S and U.S.S.R at the height of the Cold War as well as his refusal to sign the Kyoto-Protocol. Bush's unilateralism extended beyond behaving unilaterally within multilateral institutions. As Gary Prevost points out, the Bush Doctrine has come to be identified with "a policy that permits pre-emptive war against potential aggressors before they are capable of mounting attacks against the United States" (Prevost 2007:1). The notion of pre-emptive strikes, according to Prevost, is the centerpiece of a new foreign and defence policy strategy that 'allows' the U.S to engage in pre-emptive war should the U.S or its allies feel threatened by terrorists or so-called rogue states that are "engaged in the production or development of 'weapons of mass destruction'" (Prevost 2007:2). The second principle of the Bush Doctrine is most apparent through the Bush Administration's unwillingness to cooperate with and hostility toward dictatorships, 'extremist' theocratic regimes, leftist governments, populist governments as well as the attempt to establish [artificial] democracies in many of these countries.

While Latin America did not experience the full extent of the Bush administration's dogmatic foreign policy, several governments, particularly leftist populist ones, came to the attention of the Bush Administration's unilateral containment policies and democratization efforts. Since the end of the Cold

War, democratic elections in Latin America have produced several leftist governments. Yet the Bush Doctrine attempted to engage Latin America through counter-reform and counterrevolutionary strategies aimed at reversing socialist reforms. Suarez Salazar argues that the Bush Administration aimed to accomplish this goal by attempting to destabilize or overthrow leftist regimes through the promotion of bilateral trade agreements and as well as through institutional apparatuses like the United States Agency for International Development (USAID) (Salazar: 2011). According to USAID, the organization is a U.S federal agency that seeks to "extend a helping hand to those people overseas struggling to make a better life, recover from a disaster or striving to live in a free and democratic country" by providing "economic, development and humanitarian assistance around the world in support of the foreign policy goals of the United States" (USAID: 2014). While USAID for the most part is open about its biased political agenda and although its official website is filled with statistical and academic reports regarding the political economies of the nations it actively supports - Salazar points out that USAID has been used to finance private institutions such as the Center for International Private Enterprise (CIPE) and the National Endowment for Democracy (NED) in an attempt to 'strengthen' democracy within Latin America (Salazar:2011:76). Salazar argues that the Bush administration's financing of USAID, CIPE and NED has ultimately been an attempt to destabilize and roll back the constitutional governments of Bolivia, Cuba, Ecuador, Nicaragua, and Venezuela through not only the strengthening of private institutions, anti-government NGOs, anti-socialist political parties and mass disinformation media, but also through activities aimed at reducing poverty, fighting illness and supporting the development of civil society. These programs "have been geared toward counteracting the negative impact of the social programs undertaken by Cuba and Venezuela – both bilaterally and within the framework of ALBA [*Bolivarian Alliance for the Americas*] and the ALBA-Caribbean agreements" (Suarez: 2011:75). The similarity between these policies and that of U.S foreign policies toward communist states early in the Cold War era is revealing.

Carlos Olivia Campos argues that Bush's foreign policies of containment resemble a sort of continuity from Cold War era notions of the 'domino effect'. However whereas during the Cold War US leaders feared that impoverished states might turn to communism, the spread of populist socialist governments in post-Cold War Latin America has become the central source of anxiety for the US (Campos:2004:31). The Bush administration used direct and indirect methods of destabilisation in its attempts to undermine populist governments. The [failed] 2002 Venezuelan coup d'état attempt which saw the ousting of Hugo Chavez and the installing of conservative leader Pedro Carmona was ultimately linked to the Bush Administration, and while Carmona's regime only lasted 47 hours, this event tarnished the Bush Administration's reputation. While Bush publically denied any direct involvement in actually supplying the opposition with arms and money, journalists have managed to uncover information that points to the Bush Administration's awareness of the coup as well as evidence of senior level officials [of the Bush Administration] conducting discrete intelligence meetings that aimed to negotiate the terms and the methods by which Chavez would be ousted from office (Christopher: 2002). Furthermore, as Feinstein and Anne-Marie Slaughter argue, the hostility toward foreign governments (in this case Latin American populist leftist governments) "leaves almost no margin to diplomacy and forces the United States to select between promoting a change of regime or doing nothing" (Feinstein; Slaughter:2001:93). This low margin for diplomacy has translated into the use of harsh measures in dealing with leftist governments that refuse to fully comply with the U.S. Some examples include the decertification of Evo Morale's administration for not cooperating with the US in its counter-narcotic efforts which ultimately led to the removal of Bolivia from U.S trade preferences as well as the removal of US military bases from Ecuador after the refusal of President Rafael Correa to extend a bilateral trade agreement (Jonas Wolff:2011).

While the Bush administration sought to undermine leftist governments in Latin America, it placed an increased emphasis on the securitization of the remaining US regional allies, a securitization which included new de facto alliances. As Felipe de la Balze points out

> Worrying signs can be seen in the new alliances between guerilla movements and drug traffickers with the emergence of populist authoritarian regimes in countries like Venezuela and the weakening of the rule of law in the northern Andean region. The restlessness in afflicted countries could propagate and reach other countries. The political and economic influence by Washington in South America would decrease and, as a result of this, the US political, corporate and security interests could be affected (Balze:2001:70).

The Plan Colombia project largely fits the securitization initiative that Balze argues has been a major factor in American foreign policy. While Plan Colombia predates the Bush

Administration, Bush was by no means opposed to the idea of an increase in securitization (largely via military funding) with respect to Colombia. In fact, he increased the funding for Plan Colombia and the broader Andean Counterdrug Initiative to a total of $882.29 million (Serafino:2001). The Plan Colombia project promotes securitization in the form of a bilateral security agreement that aims to limit the growth of various narcotics industries. However the funds are primarily used to fight leftist insurgents and political groups that are accused of operating within the drug trafficking trade. While critics may argue that fighting leftist groups is the primary purpose of Plan Colombia and other programs like it, Rodas Chavez claims that Plan Colombia is a greater geo-economic initiative than simply a counter-insurgency and/or drug trafficking program, and that it aims to achieve a military and geopolitical sphere of influence (Chavez:2007). Chavez argues that Plan Colombia is essentially an attempt to impose the Andean Regional Initiative "as a prelude to FTAA [Free Trade Area of the Americas] to achieve this objective through bilateralism; thus Free Trade Agreements dominate the tone of US relations with many Latin American countries" (Chavez:2007:98). He adds that "in the context of neoliberal globalization, the North American regime has great interest to empower its industrial and commercial activity to the maximum, with the purpose of not repeating the accumulation crisis experienced in the recent past." (Chavez:2007:98).

While the above arguments may be theoretically biased, it must also be noted that then president of Colombia - Álvaro Uribe Vélez – used U.S economic and military aid to commit human rights violations. According to an Amnesty International report: since the start of Plan Colombia, the U.S has committed over $8 billion to the program (almost all of it going to fund military and policing institutions), leaving Colombia as "one of the largest recipients of US military aid for well over a decade and the largest within the Western Hemisphere) (Amnesty: 2013). For some time now Amnesty International has attempted to apply political pressure to stop the financing of Plan Colombia which it believes has enabled the Colombian government to pursue state sanctioned violence and human rights violations against several insurgency and political groups as well as human rights activists, journalists, unionists and academics. There is a fundamental contradiction within the Bush Doctrine when one considers that Bush himself had declared a vendetta against terrorism while his administration simultaneously supported state sanctioned violence and the terrorization of citizens. Perhaps the Bush Administration was unaware of the circumstances at the time; however a more compelling argument would be that US support of Vélez was a fundamental threat to the leftist groups active on Colombia's territory.

The Obama Doctrine

While the Bush Doctrine was placed great importance on the use of hard power as a means of reasserting U.S dominance and interests, the Obama Doctrine is more sophisticated in the sense that President Obama, unlike Bush, does not rely on a single approach to foreign policy, but rather has pursued a mixture of hard and soft power means in attempting to secure America's interest on the world stage. Obama's foreign policy can be understood as one that promotes the notion of multilateralism while still attempting to uphold and promote core democratic values. This is most apparent through (i) Obama's willingness to cooperate with multilateral institutions such as the United Nations and (ii) Obama's publically expressed distaste for leftist populist regimes – especially that of the late Hugo Chavez's. In Obama's own words:

> We know that freedom across our hemisphere must go beyond elections. In Venezuela, Hugo Chavez is a democratically elected leader. But we also know that he does not govern democratically. . . . We must put forward a vision of democracy that goes beyond the ballot box. We should increase our support for strong legislatures, independent judiciaries, free press, vibrant civil society, honest police forces, religious freedom, and the rule of law. (Obama: 2008)

Obama [like Bush] endorses the notion of 'liberal democracy' as the 'ideal' form of democracy – disregarding social democracies as illegitimate populist regimes. Salazar argues that "the redefinition of 'democracy' penned by Barack Obama aims to erode the influence of Cuba and Venezuela in the Caribbean Basin and South America". While it can be argued that such statements by scholars are overly academic and highly political, it must be noted that, if one accepts the principle of national sovereignty, the Obama Administration does not have an inherent right to essentially tell another government how to operate – especially more-so if that government has been (i) democratically elected and (ii) does not engage in human rights violations. Obama's critique of populist leftist regimes – regardless of his intentions - ultimately serves no other purpose than attempting to weaken the sphere of influence these governments may have within their respective regions.

Throughout his campaign and first term, Obama criticized Bush for "launching a misguided war in Iraq" and abandoning his pledge to make Latin America a "fundamental commitment" of his presidency (Obama: 2008). Bush's foreign policy according to Obama was "negligent toward our friends, ineffective with our adversaries, disinterested in the challenges that matter in people's lives, and incapable of advancing our interests in the region" (Obama: 2008). And whereas Bush condemned foreign governments that aided or harboured 'terrorists' or anti-American activism, Obama announced early on in his presidency that he would undertake a "direct, strong, aggressive, principled, and sustained diplomacy" towards all foreign governments, whether they are friendly, adversarial, or enemies of the United States – including reformist or anti-American governments – which according to Salazar at the time meant the members of the 'Alianza Bolivariana de los Pueblos de Nuestra América' - ALBA (English: Bolivarian Alliance of the Peoples of Our America) (Salazar:2001:74). Salazar states that;

> The destabilization or toppling of some of these governments (Bolivia, Cuba, Ecuador, Nicaragua, and Venezuela in particular) was part of the counter-reform and counterrevolutionary strategies employed by the Bush administration. In contrast to this, Obama announced that he would strengthen public diplomacy (one of the components of soft power) using Latin American immigrants living in the United States (including Cuban-Americans), increase the presence of State Department staff in Latin America and the Caribbean, and double by 2011 the official

development aid provided by the U.S. Agency for International Development (USAID) and members of the controversial Peace Corps. (Salazar:2001:74).

Obama's endorsement of the same organizations that have been attempting to destabilize leftist governments under the guise of development appears to contradict his pledge to maintain a sustained diplomatic dialogue. Further adding to this contradiction is the Obama Administration's positive reaction to the 2009 Honduran coup d'état where he recognized the legitimacy of the undemocratically selected president Porifiro Lobo without condemning the ousting of leftist leader Manuel Zelaya.

Unlike the Bush Administration's massive securitization efforts in Colombia however, the Obama Administration has reduced its budget for Plan Colombia since its first term in office (O'Gorman: 2013). This of course however could be more so the result of the 2008 financial crisis as well as the 2012 budget problem in the US than any change in foreign policy doctrine as Obama had still remained committed to Plan Colombia. In addition, Obama while abandoning his promise to renegotiate the North American Free Trade Alliance, renewed the Security and Prosperity Partnership (SPP) (which Bush promoted), which consisted of negotiations with Canada and Mexico and which seek to facilitate rather than replace bilateral trade and security agreements (Jaggers:2011). Furthermore, Obama has supported the Puebla- Panama Plan (re-named the Mesoamerican Project in 2008) as well as the Merida Initiative which aim to fight against organized crime in Central America, Haiti, the Dominican Republic, and as well as to support the Mexican government as it fights the drug trafficking war within Mexico (Torres:2008). The securitization of allied governments within the region, the recognition of emerging regional U.S allies (in the case of the Honduran coup d'état) and the financing of government agencies and institutions that aim to weaken opposition toward U.S foreign policies are some of the consistencies between the Bush and Obama Doctrines.

Changes in Latin America – A Brief Overview

While portraying himself as ideologically different from Bush, Obama has continued several of the projects undertaken by Bush's Administration. It is still uncertain why Obama chose to approach Latin America with a greater emphasis on soft power, public diplomacy and economic coordination, while simultaneously maintaining the use of Bush era (or traditional U.S) hard power tactics within the region. Most theoretical frameworks [if not all] can only provide limited insight into such questions. What is certain is that being the political leader and military commander in chief of a regional and arguably global hegemonic is no easy task and more often than not requires adapting and responding to the ideological and policy shifts within specific regions or nations of interest so as to maintain America's own national security and political economic "interests" on the world stage. This paper maintains that the shift in policymaking and policy implementation from the Bush to the Obama era can be understood through not only the broader theoretical framework of neo-Gramscianism, but also through an understanding of the political, economic and ideological shift within several Latin American and Caribbean countries. In other words, the continuities of policies from the Bush Doctrine can be best understood by critically analyzing not the partisan shifts within the US, but rather the ideological changes within several

Latin American countries as these changes have essentially pressured US policymakers to make an effort to re-engage the Latin American region.

The regional political, economic and ideological shifts that occurred within several Latin American countries during the early 2000s are often cited as a response to the decades of the imposition of the neoliberal Washington Consensus and free trade exploitation.[26] Under the leadership of Hugo Chavez and Evo Morales (perhaps with the exception of Fidel Castro and Raul Castro) several leftist Latin American political groups were able to establish themselves as legitimate social-democratic regimes [The Pink Tide]. In 2004 Hugo Chavez founded ALBA as an alternative to the FTAA agreement proposed by the U.S, and in a few short years the membership grew to a total of nine members. Honduras withdrew after the coup d'état which saw the promotion of conservative leader Roberto Micheletti to de facto president, and later Lobo as elected president. While ALBA currently has a membership of eight Latin American countries out of the total nineteen within the region, the organization has mounted a fundamental and unprecedented challenge to the presence, influence and control of the US within and over the region. Other challenges have included Hugo Chavez's somewhat facetious anti-U.S speeches in the UN and the formation of hard economic power institutions such as Banco del Sur (Bank of the South). As Wesley C. Marshall and Louis-Philippe Rochon (2010:187) outline, there was a brief period (in the 1990s) in which the Latin American region enjoyed capital inflows that "corresponded to

---

[26] See Kaltwasser (2010)) *Moving Beyond the Washington Consensus: The Resurgence of the Left in Latin America* & Marshall and Rochon (2010) *Financing economic development in Latin America: the Banco del Sur.* Journal of Post Keynesian Economics

the privatization of the largest state-owned companies of the region". From 1998 to 2005 however the region experienced massive outflows of capital, "due in large part to the repatriation of profits to the headquarters of multinational corporations (MNCs) that benefited from privatizations in the region" (Vidal, 2007). In an effort to reverse the pervasive effects of foreign investments and borrowing from international financial and lending institutions like the International Monetary Fund (IMF) and World Bank (WB), the Banco del Sur was proposed as an alternative for the countries of the Latin American and Caribbean region.

The bank (which began functioning in 2013) aims to be both a regional development bank and a regional monetary regulator in an attempt to both develop the region without major foreign aid as well as dissociating itself from greater dependency on the international market through the installation of a proposed regional currency (the SUCRE) while simultaneously attempting to reduce the use of the US dollar (USD); this trend has been dubbed the 'de-dollarization' of the region (Marshall; Rochan:2010). Accompanying this de-dollarization is an overall shift away from US supported institutions that ALBA suspects of attempting to weaken or drain the region; this is generally evident in the increased willingness of ALBA countries to do business with emerging powers like China. While the US presence within the region remains strong, it is weakening as more nations are reducing their dependence on the American market: from the commodities markets within the private sphere to nationalized oil companies (in the case of Venezuela and Ecuador) to the negotiation of the terms for borrowing funds, and a diversification of foreign direct investments, Latin American countries, particularly ALBA countries, have engaged the international system more than ever (Cerna:2011). It appears, therefore that Olivia Campos's theory of the domino effect taking place within contemporary Latin America is not the most unreasonable of predictions.

Theoretical Framework and Conclusion

In the early 1980s Robert Cox had inadvertently developed a new model of Marxian analysis of the global political economy through re-interpreting Italian political theorist Antonio Gramsci's theories of hegemony within capitalist societies and borrowing key principles from Niccolò Machiavelli (Cox:1983). Neo-Gramscianism like other Marxian theories critiques bourgeois culture and places materialist gains and the effects of capital accumulation at the heart of societal ills. However unlike most Marxian theories neo-Gramscianism redefined several traditionally 'realist' terms such as 'hegemony', 'status quo' and 'power' by adding a materialist conceptualization as well as placing a greater emphasis on institutional hegemony rather than simply physical power. What makes this particular framework a useful model of analysis for understanding the continuities within the Bush and Obama Doctrine as well as the ideological shift within Latin America is that while neo-Gramscian theory recognizes several of the theoretical frameworks outlined within traditional international relations theories, the arguments proposed by neo-Gramscians are innately contemporary in their critique as they acknowledge the changes that have taken place in a post-globalized world. First and foremost, unlike the structural realist (or neorealist) models of hegemony that place the 'anarchical' nature of the international system at the heart of conflict and state pursuits or classical realist models that place it on the more ambiguous notion of 'human nature' – neo-

Gramscians emphasize the reinforcement of existing historical economic 'blocs' and institutions through coercive policies as the main source of conflict within the international system. According to neo-Gramscians, institutional economic or 'historical' blocs (which constitute a hierarchical class structure that is characterized through the juxtaposition of economic, political, ethnic and ideological spheres of activity) - can only be established when a dominant hegemonic social class, or in the case of the broader international system a group of nations - maintains cohesion and identity within the bloc through the "propagation of a common culture" (Cox: 1983:168). In regards to Latin America, this is evident through not only the U.S attempt to bind the region to American style political and economic models of governance and growth through the promotion of liberalism, democracy, neoliberalism, and free market capitalism, policies that also include the US promotion of regional free trade agreements. The US has also shown an unwillingness to accept the existence of social populist democracies in favour of traditional, conservative liberal democracies as well as conservative authoritarian regimes that strategically ally themselves with the US. This represents an attempt to reinforce 'American' values as common to all as well as maintain their geopolitical interests. The attempt to destabilize social populist democracies through hard power initiatives further highlights the attempt to maintain the economic status quo.

According to the Neo-Gramscian theorist Stephen Gill the existing historical blocs since the emergence of globalization have been characterized by the restructuring of capital, liberalization of markets and an overall political shift to the right (Gill: 1995:400). Within the Americas this shift occurred with the implementation of the Washington Consensus (which is generally accepted among scholars of several fields as an attempt to spread or enforce -

depending on the interpretation - neoliberal economic policies of austerity measures, de-unionization, de-regulation, privatization, tax reform and conservative fiscal policies). Gill further argues the increased emphasis on neoliberal economic policies represents an ideological shift among policymakers who now believe it is imperative to enable an ideal environment for the free market to flourish as the market economy is understood to be necessary to the progress of human culture and civilization. Gill along with other scholars label this ideological phenomenon as the 'market civilization' (Gill: 1995:399). In order for the free market to flourish not only must states accept free market enterprises, but they must also be committed to the very notion of free enterprise. The nationalization of oil, gas as well as several other industries that range from energy to the agricultural by the Latin American Left represents a direct threat to the establishment of the hegemonic market status quo as they distort markets.

Cox notes that Gramsci argued historical blocs are prone to experience an 'organic crisis'; whereby there is a 'crisis of authority' within the ruling class's hegemony by a counter-hegemonic bloc that aims to restructure established ideas, institutions, and material capacities (Cox: 1983:167). Cox adds that if new-counter-hegemonic blocs are to succeed (i) a subordinate class – often under the leadership of a charismatic individual (Gramsci uses the term 'Ceaserism' to describe such an individual) must "establish its hegemony over other subordinate classes" and (ii) "this process requires intensive dialogue between leaders and followers within the would-be hegemonic class". In the case of Latin America, several of the events of the last decade do indeed coincide with the aforementioned notions; for the rise of socialism does require one subordinate group (the proletariat or worker) to assert its hegemony over other subordinate groups such as the farmer and others disenfranchised within the nation-state. Coincidentally Cox explicitly uses the worker and farmer as an example within his argument. The relative success of the new bloc within the organic crisis however can also be attributed to the success of charismatic leftist leaders – particularly the late Hugo Chavez; in fact, the very definition of populism holds the charisma of a popular leader to be imperative to their success.

Some may argue that the Washington Consensus and the consequent neoliberal globalization policies created an environment which facilitated US political economic hegemony; the U.S has not entirely abandoned traditional modes of hegemonic enforcement and has not abandoned its securitization efforts as a means to reinforce institutional structures or punishing governments, political groups or insurgents that aimed to challenge it. It took decades for a reformist movement to gain enough success to formally challenge the status quo. In summary, the Latin American Left in recent years has been behaving counter-hegemonically – whereas the U.S has been behaving hegemonically. This fact is most evident in the post 9/11 era under Bush and again with the establishment of Leftist strongholds during the late 2000s when Obama was president.

This paper maintains that while Neo-Gramscian theory does not have all the answers for explaining the international political economy of Latin America, or why leaders of superpower states behave hegemonically, the theory does give some insight as to why Obama's foreign policy within the region has largely shifted away from the draconian hard power strategies that were implemented by Bush, to a "smart strategy" that utilizes a mixture of soft and hard power. This shift by Obama in the end is essentially a new engagement strategy that aims to peacefully and simultaneously dissuade the region from leftist political-economic aspirations while simultaneously enabling an environment for free market enterprise to flourish. But that in itself is a topic for another paper.

BIBLIOGRAPHY

Amnesty International (2012) "Colombia."
<www.amnesty.org/en/region/colombia/report-2012>

Balze de la, Felipe. (2001) Searching for Allies in the Backyard: the TLCAN and the Southern Cone. Foreign Affairs in Spanish

BBC News. (2002) "US denies backing Chavez plotters"
<http://news.bbc.co.uk/2/hi/americas/193

Campos Olivia, Carlos. (2007) The United States – Latin America and the Caribbean: From Neopan-Americanism to the American System for the Twenty-First Century

Cerna , Michael. (2011) "China Research Center | China's Growing Presence in Latin America: Implications for U.S. and Chinese Presence in the Region." China Research Center.
<http://www.chinacenter.net/chinas-growing-presence-in-latin-america-implications-for-u-s-

Chavez Rodas, German (2007) Plan Colombia – A Key Ingredient in the Bush Doctrine. New York: Palgrave MacMillian

Cox, Robert. (1981) Social Forces, States and World Orders: Beyond International Relations Theory. Millennium Journal of International Studies

Cox, Robert. (1983) Gramsci, Hegemony and International Relations: An Essay in Method. Millennium Journal of International Studies Feinstein, Lee and Slaughter, Annie-Marie (2001) The Obligation of Preventing. Foreign Affairs in Spanish

Gill, Stephen. (1995) Globalisation, Market Civilisation, and Disciplinary Neoliberalism. Millennium Journal of International Studies

Halper, Stefan and Jonathan Clarke. (2004) America Alone: The Neo-Conservatives and the Global Order. Cambridge University Press.

Jaggers Stanfield, Tyler .(2011) NAFTA and the SPP: An Unfinished System.

Kaltwasser Rovira, Cristobal. (2010) Moving Beyond the Washington Consensus: The Resurgence of the Left in Latin America. Internationale Politik und Gesellschaft

Kaltwasser Rovira, Cristobal. (2011) Toward Post-Neoliberalism in Latin America?. Latin American Research Review, Latin American Studies Association

Marquis, Christopher. (2002) "Bush Officials Met With Venezuelans Who Ousted Leader." New York Times

Marshall C. Wesley and Rochon, Louis-Philippe (2010) Financing economic development in Latin America: the Banco del Sur. Journal of Post Keynesian Economics

Obama, Barack (2008) "Renewing U.S. Leadership in the Americas"

O'Gorman , Joey. (2013) "Obama cuts funds to combat Colombia's drug trade Colombia News. <http://colombiareports.com/obama-cuts-funds-to-combat-colombias-drug-trade/>.

Prevost, Gary and Campos Olivia, Carlos. (2002) Neoliberalism and Neopanamericanism: The View from Latin America. New York: Palgrave MacMillian

Prevost, Gary and Campos Olivia, Carlos. (2007) The Bush Doctrine and Latin America. New York: Palgrave MacMillian.

Rodriguez Torres, Sarah . (2008) Del Plan Puebla-Panamá al Proyecto Mesoamérica. Centro de Investigaciones de la Economía Internacional.

Salazar Suarez, Luis. (2011) Obama's "Smart Strategies" against Latin America and the Caribbean Continuities and Changes. Latin American Perspectives Journal

Serafino M, Nina (2001) Colombia: Plan Colombia Legislation and
Assistance. CRS Report for Congress
USAID. (2014) "U.S. Agency for International Development." U.S.
Agency for International Development.

Wolff, Jonas. (2011) Re-engaging Latin America's Left? US relations
with Bolivia and Ecuador from Bush to Obama. Peace Research
Institute Frankfurt.

11. US FOREIGN POLICY IMPLEMENTATION IN GADDAFI-ERA LIBYA

By: Daniel Bodistean

Timeline of Events

1951
- Libya gains independence from colonial powers under King Idris al- Sanusi

1969
- King Idris is deposed in a military coup by Col Muammar Gaddafi who seeks a socialist pan-Arab agenda. The oil industry is nationalized along with other key industries.

1970
- American and British airbases are closed and the property of foreign nationals is nationalised.

1973-1977
- Gaddafi creates a cultural and "people's revolution"

1978
- The first sanctions are imposed by the US, banning the sale of arms to Libya.

1981
- The US shoots down Libyan jets.

1982
- President Regan uses a section of the *Trade Expansion Act of 1962* to boycott imports of Libyan crude and exports of oil production technology.

1986
- After a bombing of a disco in Berlin, which killed an American soldier, President Regan puts in place trade and financial control sanctions against Libya. The US also bombs Libyan military facilities

1988
- Lockerbie Bombing takes places, where Libyan agents allegedly blew up an airliner

1989
- UTA Flight 772 is blown up over the Sahara Dessert, once again allegedly linked to Gaddafi

1992
- UNSC imposes sanctions against Libya over the two bombings

2003
- Gaddafi attempts rapprochement with the west through various avenues

2011
- Anti Gaddafi uprisings begin in Libya, resulting in Gaddafi's death in October

The appearance of Muammar Gadhafi as the new Libyan leader following a coup that he orchestrated in 1969 with the help of his Revolutionary Command Council brought a new and troublesome state actor into the world as seen from Washington. The socialist Islamist nature of Gadhafi's politics, his sponsoring of international terrorism and his insistence on the creation of a nuclear programme, despite the fact that Libya had ratified the NPT, all posed significant foreign policy issues for the USA. With the support of some of its allies, the US adopted a policy of containment and isolation toward the Gadhafi regime for most of that regime's existence, though there was some change during the regime's later years, after it in turn had also modified its policies (The Guardian 2011). The Gadhafi case is important because it is touted as a success for the US, which seemed to have achieved all of its official objectives, such as the cessation of the Libyan nuclear program and the regime's decision not only to cease the support of terrorism, but also to pay damages for previous incidents of Libyan-supported terrorist acts (Davenport 2014). In the end, the Gadhafi regime itself ceased to exist, though the extent to which this was a foreign policy objective of the US is subject to debate (Schumacher 1986).

This essay will analyse the foreign policy of the United States concerning Libya by means of chronological review of events. Such an approach will allow me to divide the study into periods of time in which the US attempted different, yet specific methods of foreign policy implementation. The implementation of American foreign policy has relied on three principal means, which can be described by three short labels: a stick, carrot and finally a gun method. The stick describes the initial period of sanctions which the USA implemented after 1978, followed by a period of removal of those sanctions and the adoption of various incentives after

2004. Finally the period of military action (the gun) followed, terminating the Gaddafi regime in 2011 (USA Engage 2012). Though I have assigned a label to each of the three time periods, there are no clear black and white lines delineating these periods and at times there may have been an overlap, where more than one method was used simultaneously.

It is important to define the objectives of American foreign policy as they are the independent variables. The extent to which these objectives were achieved will be a measure of the dependent variables, whilst the independent (exogenous, as this essay does not treat foreign policy decision making) variables are the particular actions, and forms, through which the USA implemented its foreign policy. Each stage of time will be analysed in context, measuring the extent of success of each type of foreign policy implemented by first aggregating and analysing the various actions taken by the US (the independent variables) and finally analysing the outcomes of these actions by examining whether the policy objectives at the time were achieved (the dependent variable). The conclusion of this analysis will attempt to look at the overall success of each implementation type (for each time period) and will attempt to analyse to what extent they led to the overall success or failure of the implementation of US foreign policy.

Trade and Economic sanctions

The period between the first sanctions in 1978 and the removal of those sanctions two decades later included several objectives of US foreign policy. The first official reason was to punish Libya for being a sponsor of terrorism worldwide, presumably in an attempt to stop such future actions by the Libyan government (Hufbauer et al 2001). The removal of Gaddafi from power has been cited as another intention of US foreign policy throughout the regime's lifetime (Schumacher 1986). There is little evidence of any other US foreign policy objectives during this first period. The US sought to punish the regime and isolate it, rather than induce it to take any specific actions. Any leverage gained and concessions won during this period seem to have been accidental and not actively sought by the US government.

Background

The rise of Muammar Gaddafi to power in 1969 put a number of western nations in an uneasy position as they had supported the previous regime led by the pro-Western King Idris. Despite this unease and the fact that Gaddafi nationalised the assets of BP (a large British owned oil company), the United States did not impose its first sanctions against Libya until 1978, when it banned the sales of military equipment. This was followed by the addition of Libya to a newly created list of states that sponsor terrorism, which came with a number of economic sanctions. In 1982, President Reagan used a section of the *Trade Expansion Act of 1962* to boycott imports of Libyan crude oil and embargo exports of oil production technology. This was followed by the prohibition of all refined petroleum imports in 1985. Following the bombing and death of a US soldier in a Berlin discotheque in 1986, President Regan used the *International Emergency Economic Powers Act* (IEEPA) to put in place trade and financial control sanctions against Libya, prohibiting exports of most goods and services and loans and credits to the Libyan government, as well as freezing Libyan government assets in U.S. banks. This was followed by the State Department order to U.S. oil companies to sell their holdings in Libya in 1986 (USA Engage 2012). The

Lockerbie and Air France bombing of flights which occurred in 1988 and 1989 respectively and which were linked to Gaddafi caused governments other than those of the US to impose similar economic sanctions. Through the UN, the US pushed and achieved a Security Council resolution in 1992, which put in force an arms embargo and the prohibition of all travel to and from Libya. This was followed by a ban on the sale of petroleum equipment and the freezing of all non-petroleum related Libyan government assets abroad the following year (Davenport 2014). Finally it is of interest to note that during 1986 the Reagan administration took a number of military actions, including the shooting down of two Libyan jets and an air raid that killed one of Gadhafi's daughters in her crib. In other words, at this time the US used military action as well at covert intelligence actions, in addition to economic sanctions, in attempts to destabilise the regime (Schumacher 1986).

We can now attempt to assess the success of the implementation measures (the dependent variable) used by the US during this first time period. As so often occurs, the measure of success of the outputs depends on the time frame used. A time frame looking at the 1980s for example would point to an at least partial failure in the foreign policy objectives of the US. The Lockerbie and Air France bombings might be viewed as evidence of escalating terrorist actions despite the implementation of sanctions against Libya. A longer view of events which takes into account the 1980s and the 1990s would encompass the handing over of the two Lockerbie suspects, which could be viewed as a successful response to the sanctions imposed by the US and the ones that were imposed by other governments. The handover of the two suspects to the Dutch for trial can be viewed as directly linked to the sanctions; as part of the deal was to have the 1992

Security Council sanctions suspended immediately after the handover (Davenport 2014). Even in this longer view of time, the destabilisation of the regime itself and the bringing about of a coup did not occur. It seems that the economic sanctions had little effect on the stability of the Gaddafi regime during this time period. Overall, the implementation of US policy through economic and trade sanctions seemed to be effective in stopping the state sponsoring of terrorism, which was the explicit and urgent objective of US foreign policy. The US, however, did not achieve its other objective, which was to overthrow the Gaddafi regime.

Positive inducement diplomacy

A foreign policy objective that was pertinent and instrumental in US foreign policy of the post 2000 period was the enforcement of a global anti-WMD regime. The Libyan nuclear program was of particular interest for the first George W. Bush administration. This was evident before 9/11, but became more pronounced with the 2003 invasion of Iraq (Nuclear Threat Initiative 2012). The anti-terrorism campaign also became far more pertinent in the new millennium, as the terrorist acts in New York led to an overly sensitive American public. These two objectives dominated the American foreign policy agenda of the time and became main objectives as it became clear that the Gaddafi regime was ready to cooperate on the issue (Zoubir 2011). The ousting of Gaddafi became less of an issue as it became clear that Libya in its current form could become an important ally in the fight against terrorism; yet the change of the regime might also be seen as a continuing objective (Zoubir 2011). This is an illustration of how a means of implementation can become bureaucratically embedded and survive the objectives which it was originally intended to achieve.

The gradual switch from negative to positive inducements as the US attempted to eradicate terrorism and remove the WMD threat from Libya is believed to have begun with negotiations as early as 1999. Despite the fact that Libya was offering to negotiate the destruction of its chemical weapons, the US government refused to negotiate in secret talks until there was a settlement and admission of fault to previous terrorist acts, namely Lockerbie. The pursuit of those narrow objectives led Libya to continue the development of its WMD program, with US intelligence agencies becoming aware of an international ring linked to Pakistan which sought to export nuclear material to Libya as early as 2000 (Davenport 2014). Days before the Iraq invasion in 2003, Gaddafi had his agents approach western powers, namely the US and UK, in an attempt to negotiate the dismantling of Libya's WMD programs. Later that year Libya accepted responsibility for the Lockerbie bombing and paid a large sum as recompense to the families affected. This led to further removal of Security Council sanctions against Libya. During that same year a US ship also intersected a cargo ship carrying nuclear material to Libya, in effect leading to the dismantling of Libya's supply chain of nuclear material and to the admission and opening of the Gaddafi regime's numerous nuclear sites to foreign observers (Nuclear Threat Initiative 2012). After the official declaration ending its pursuit of nuclear weapons, Libya saw a reprieve from the US itself, which, under President Bush in 2004, declared the end to the national emergency related to Libya. At this time an Executive Order was signed declaring the resumption of normal commerce with Libya, terminating the previous sanctions imposed since the 1980s. Libya remained on the terrorist list until 2006, but diplomatic relations and resumption of normal economic interaction were already in place by 2008 (USA Engage 2012).

The implementation approach used by the US during this time can be described as one of positive inducements in attempt to nurture a new relationship with the Gaddafi regime. The gradual removal of the previous sanctions against the regime could be seen as incentives to Gaddafi for his actions. Although the US seems to have achieved its objectives more efficiently during this period, there is a difficulty establishing a link between the actions taken and the results. Here once again multiple factors were at play in US policy implementation, including the use of intelligence agencies in the October 2003 seizure of a ship with centrifuge-related cargo and the collapse of the supply chain on which Gaddafi depended on for nuclear fuel (Nuclear Threat Initiative 2012). However, positive inducements remained the major method through which the US sought to pursue its policy. Despite the fact that incentives, such as the removal of trade restrictions, were used as a method for foreign policy achievements, it has been argued that a more pertinent cause of the disarmament done by Gaddafi was the fear that he might have been the next Saddam. Zoubir (2011) argues that it was coercive diplomacy, the threat of action, which, after the US invasion in Iraq, led Gaddafi to change course. Interestingly Zoubir also argues that US policy achieved a change in Libya's course on terrorism, but failed to affect the nature of the regime itself, a policy objective of the US government. Therefore, whilst a level of correlation could be observed between the tit-for-tat removal of sanctions and the successful achievement of some policy objectives success, it is difficult to ascertain that this was the cause for the change.

Military action

The uprisings which began in Libya in early 2011 as part of the overall Arab-Spring marked a new era in US foreign policy toward the Gaddafi regime. Despite the normalisation of relations prior to the fact, the US was faced with a tough choice in what its objectives should be in the future. As the fighting in Libya grew more intense and human rights abuses became apparent, the objectives of the US shifted from one of cooperation on terrorism matters to the change in regime type within Libya. While the Security Council resolution under which the NATO military action, which led to the ousting of the Gaddafi regime was not intended for regime change, it can be rather easily ascertained that the US foreign policy objectives of the time were, as stated by President Obama, that "it is US policy that Gaddafi needs to go" (the Guardian 2011). While terrorism was still an overall concern for the US government, by 2011, Libya and the Gaddafi regime represented an ally in the fight against terrorism. This was a far cry from previous decades' policy and hence it can be deduced that the fight against terrorism was no longer an objective as it pertained to Libya (Zoubir 2011). The dismantling of all WMD projects was also well underway (Nuclear Threat Initiative 2012).

At the onset of violence in Libya the US assumed the position that it would seek to protect civilians from violence caused by the regime. In February 2011, President Obama invoked IEEPA once again and signed an Executive Order, which led to the imposition of new sanctions against the Gaddafi regime. These sanctions were more specific than previous ones had been and sought to target specific members of the regime and institutions which were believed to be linked to Gaddafi (USA Engage 2012). The US, in conjunction with the UK, sought the implementation of a no-fly zone over Libya, which would in effect permit military action in the country. Security Council resolution 1973 was adopted in March of 2011 (UNSC 2011) under which NATO executed 26,000 sorties, destroyed 5900 targets of which 600 included tanks and armoured vehicles (BBC 2011). Under heavy fire, Gaddafi lost Tripoli by August of that year, finally being captured and killed in October (Nuclear Threat Initiative 2012).

The initial US objective was regime change, which successive American presidents saw as preferable; in 2011, they achieved this objective by using military action. The fall of the Gaddafi regime could be directly linked to the implementation of the no-fly zone, which blocked Gaddafi from effectively using his air force in maintaining his regime. The success of bringing down the regime would appear to have achieved the maximum US objective. Yet this success was more apparent than real. As demonstrated by the attack on the US embassy and the subsequent murder of the US ambassador in Benghazi on September 11, 2012, the fall of Gaddafi represented a step back. The US was once again the target of terrorism originating in Libya (Doornbos, Moussa 2012). While military action seems to have been most effective in achieving the objective of regime change, it put in jeopardy other possible foreign policy objectives sought by the US.

Conclusion

The overall effects of US policy implementation measures during the Gaddafi era, including economic and trade sanctions, positive inducements and military action, have been ambivalent result in regards to US foreign policy objectives. The main objectives over the span of the Gaddafi regime were the end of terrorist action and of the sponsorship of terrorism, the end of the nuclear and other WMD programs and finally the end of the regime itself. Whilst the end of the Gaddafi regime signaled an accomplishment of the initial goal sought by presidents as early as Reagan, it would be simplistic to say that the US achieved its foreign policy objectives. The various implementation techniques chosen led to variant results for each policy objective. The imposition of sanctions and trade barriers during the regime's early years brought about the end of terrorist actions and of the sponsorship of terrorism by Gaddafi, but failed to bring about the regime change sought in the early 80s. The subsequent carrot approach permitted the US to achieve the nuclear disarmament of Libya and allowed for what some have called an ally in the fight against terrorism. Finally, the military action taken as part of NATO led to the end of the regime, an initial objective, but that in turn led to instability and a resurgence of terrorism. Overall, it seems US policy was effective in establishing and achieving the objectives it set itself one at a time, at times putting at risk previous achievements in order to pursue what the current administration deems the most important objective.

The implementation of the final policy, and others before it, put strain on the causal link between US policy and Libyan reaction. The presence of other countries' foreign policy implementation measures throughout Gaddafi's reign makes it difficult to distinguish the extent to which it was the US action which achieved the objectives. Further research on this subject should attempt to operationalise the variables, attempting to give numerical values and measurements to each independent and dependant variable. It is conceivable that with proper coding and data, a regression analysis would yield more informative regarding the efficacy of each policy implementation measure and a clearer assessment of the effect of US foreign policy on Libya during this period.

BIBLIOGRAPHY

Abulof, Uriel (2013). Nuclear Diversion Theory and Legitimacy Crisis: The Case of Iran. *Politics & Policy* **41: 5**: 690-722.

Gary Clyde Hufbauer, Jeffrey J. Schott, Kimberly Ann Elliott, assisted by Barbara Oegg (2001). Using Sanctions to Fight Terrorism. *Institute for International Economics.* Available at: http://www.iie.com/publications/pb/print.cfm?ResearchId=79&doc=pub. Accessed April 1, 2013.

Bates, Stephen (2011). Muammar Gaddafi timeline. *The Guardian.* Available at: http://www.theguardian.com/world/2011/oct/20/muammar-gaddafi-timeline. Accessed April 2, 2013.

BBC News Africa (2011). Libya no-fly zone: Coalition firepower. *British Broadcasting Corporation.* Available at: http://www.bbc.com/news/world-africa-12806112. Accessed April 1, 2013.

Davenport, Kelsey (2014). Chronology of Libya's Disarmament and Relations with the United States. *Arms Control Association.* Available at: http://www.armscontrol.org/factsheets/LibyaChronology. Accessed April 2, 2013.

Doornbos, Harald and Moussa Jenan (2012). "Troubling" Surveillance before Benghazi Attack. *Foreign Policy.* November 1, 2012. Available at: http://www.foreignpolicy.com/articles/2012/11/01/troubling_surveillance_before_benghazi_attack. Accessed April 2, 2013.

El-Khawas, Mohamed (1989).Libya's foreign policy under Gaddafi. *Africa Today.* **36:3/4**: 121-123. Retrieved from http://search.proquest.com.ezproxy.library.yorku.ca/docview/197469135?accountid=15182. Accessed April 2, 2013.

MacAskill, Ewen (2011). Obama hails death of Muammar Gaddafi as foreign policy success. *The Guardian.* Available at: http://www.theguardian.com/world/2011/oct/20/obama-hails-death-gaddafi. Accessed April 2, 2013.

Nordenman, Magnus (2013). The End of the War on Terror and the Future of US Counterterrorism. *Mediterranean Quarterly* **24: (3).** Available at: http://muse.jhu.edu.ezproxy.library.yorku.ca/journals/mediterranean _quarterly/v024/24.3.nordenman.html. Accessed April 2, 2013.

Nuclear Threat Initiative (2012). Country Profiles: Libya. *Nuclear Threat Initiative.* Available at: http://www.nti.org/country-profiles/libya/nuclear/. Accessed April 2, 2013.

Sawani, Youssef (2012). Post-Qadhafi Libya: interactive dynamics and the political future. *Contemporary Arab Affairs* **5:1**: 1-26. Accessed through JSTOR. Accessed April 2, 2013.

Schumacher, Edward (1986) The United States and Libya. *Foreign Affairs.* December 1, 1986.Available at: http://www.foreignaffairs.com/articles/41701/edward-schumacher/the-united-states-and-libya. Accessed April 2, 2014.

United Nations Security Council (2011). Security Council Approves 'No-Fly Zone' Over Libya, Authorizing 'All Necessary measures' To Protect Civilians, By Vote Of 10 In Favour With 5 Abstentions (17 March 2011). *UNSC.* Available at: https://www.un.org/News/Press/docs/2011/sc10200.doc.htm. Accessed April 1, 2013.

USA Engage (2012). U.S. Foreign Policy Sanctions: Libya. *National Foreign Trade Council.* Available at: http://usaengage.org/Issues/Sanctions-Programs/Libya/ . Accessed April 2, 2013.

Zoubir, Yahia (2011). The United States and Libya: the limits of coercive diplomacy. *The Journal of North African Studies* **16: 2**: 275–29